The Fire Within

To my new friend Nancy,

Blessings,

Marie McGale

D1598264

The Fire Within

Connect Your Gifts with Your Calling

MARCIA MALZAHN

Library of Congress Control Number: 2015914745
ISBNs: 978-0-9967971-0-8 (paperback); 978-0-9967971-1-5 (ePub);
978-0-9967971-2-2 (Kindle)

Editing: Marly Cornell
Book Design: Ryan Scheife
Cover Design: Ryan Scheife
Cover Painting: Isa Tyler

Malzahn Publishing
Maple Grove, Minnesota, U.S.A.

CONTENTS

INTRODUCTION

I found my life's purpose. And I want to help you find yours. I am using the term "purpose," but others may call it a mission, a passion, a dream, a calling, a reason for being, or perhaps the answer to the question, "Why am I here?" It doesn't matter what you call it; what matters is the desire to feel useful, needed by others, and to make a positive difference in the world. Helping others is the bottom line, regardless of the specific calling. I firmly believe that we are all called on by God to help others, but we each have to find our own niche.

My mission in life is to help working people be successful in every area of their lives. But it took me years to discover that mission. My first step was figuring out what my actual God-given gifts were. As I began to recognize my own gifts, I found an intimate relationship between what I love doing and what I'm good at. I am better at things that are a combination of my interests and some natural talents. Certain abilities that I possess help me do certain particular functions or tasks well. Finally identifying those talents led me to explore areas of work where I can use them well.

Every adult person works, one way or another. What kind of work and whether a person is paid for the work is a different issue. Either way, everybody works. I have had a full-time job outside of my home since before I came to America, with only brief time off when I had my children. The stories in this book are from my own experiences throughout my life as a working person and as a Christian person of faith, first discovering my gifts and then my calling.

Though I don't pretend to know exactly what might inspire other people to discover their life purpose or mission, I hope that my story will help inspire you to consider yours. Whether you work inside or outside of your home, whether you are paid or not for the work you do, this book has a message for you. The message is a spiritual one and a practical one. I want to encourage and motivate you to recognize your gifts, polish them, and use them to help others.

I have already explained that my purpose is to help working people be successful in every area of their lives. What is your purpose?

Part 1

————◄•►————

YOUR GIFTS

The Discovery Process

Chapter 1

Gifts among Us

One day I was at a store looking for items to decorate my new house, because I was preparing for a party at night with my coworkers. I looked and looked, but no ideas came to my mind. I asked myself, *What do people buy to make their houses look pretty and stylish? How do people imagine what colors match and what knick-knacks look good together?* I don't know. In my state of desperation I asked God, "Lord, please give me the gift of home decorating. I don't have that one."

I heard no answer, but I instantly thought of calling my sister who does have the gift of home decorating. She loves doing that with her house and everyone else's. My sister answered the phone, which was a relief since I was almost in tears at that point, feeling sorry for myself and feeling the pressure that my house wasn't going to look as good as I wanted it.

She immediately started giving me ideas of what items to buy, and in what colors, and how they would go together. She offered to come to my house to decorate before the party. I agreed with great relief in my heart.

My sister came the next day with a basket full of items—tablecloths, beautiful wreaths, silk flowers, and fall leaves that she placed gracefully in strategic places so the leaves would look their best. She set up the paper plates, cups, silverware, and fall-color bowls around my kitchen island. Everything looked beautiful. The party was a success. My guests really enjoyed my home and said how everything looked so pretty and inviting.

Meanwhile, I had a revelation about how God gives us gifts: He distributes His gifts (including the gift of home decorating) among all His people, so that we need each other and will work together. This idea made perfect sense. If He had given me all the gifts that everybody else has, I would not need anybody else, or Him for that matter. I would have it all in me. That is not God's intention. God made me realize that I actually do have all the gifts. They are just not all inside of me. They are distributed among all people He puts in my path.

I learned several key points with this lesson: 1) I will probably not acquire the gift of home decorating, because He already gave me many other gifts; 2) God wants me to enjoy that particular gift through the talents of others; 3) I must be humble enough to recognize that I don't have some gifts and ask for help when needed; 4) We all need to recognize the gifts within us, so we are ready to share them with others when needed. Those gifts are for us to enjoy and for us to share with those around us. Isn't God's masterful plan wonderful?

This interior design lesson is one of many small experiences I have had with the Lord in my daily routines that I cannot disregard. When my sister came to my house that day, she was in her talent territory, enjoying every moment of decorating my house. She even said she would enjoy doing this sort of work for a living, but she did it for me for free. In the end, we were both blessed. She enjoyed a break from her daily routine, and the entire experience was a great help to me.

When I shared this story in my women's prayer group, people paid close attention and felt relieved to know they don't have to have every skill either. Together we realized that the "perfect" woman of Proverbs 31 doesn't exist in one person. Each of us is that perfect woman in God's eyes when we share and utilize each other's gifts and put them to use together. To try to be like the woman in Proverbs 31 (read the entire chapter and you will see what I mean) can be intimidating, because she is perfect. Everything she does prospers. She has her household under control at all times. She is well-kept and in shape, works hard from morning to night, and her family is always well fed and clothed. Who can do all that these days? I doubt that women living during that time in the Bible did everything the Proverbs 31 woman did, either. God shows us how to enjoy and use all the gifts He gave us as women and as sisters in Christ.

The same lesson applies to men. God distributes all the attributes of being a perfect husband, worker, father, brother, and everything else among all men. Men have the same requirement to be humble and recognize their gifts and when they need help from others. They need to understand that it is okay to ask for help when needed.

Each person would benefit from taking an honest inventory of each gift and perhaps each area needing help, so that we can readily share our talents with others and understand what things we need help with. People are blessed to have the opportunity to help others. By asking others for help, we give them a sense of purpose as well. Every person enjoys a sense of feeling needed, which helps them know they are valuable.

We would find more satisfaction in the workplace if, in addition to sharing the gifts we have, we asked for help more often and surrounded ourselves with the people who possess the gifts we are lacking. God knows what He's doing. He knows the types of people He put together to work together and share their gifts. It is our job to stop and recognize who those people are and how we can work together better with one another. This formula builds strong teams and organizations, which in turn creates successful companies.

---

1 CORINTHIANS 1:4 (NLT) *I always thank my God for you and for the gracious gifts he has given you, now that you belong to Christ Jesus.*

• **QUESTIONS TO PONDER**
   1. Do you display the humility to ask for help in the areas you are not gifted in?
   2. Do you recognize the gifts God places around you?
   3. What are you doing to utilize the gifts God gave you through other people?

• **ACTION ITEMS**
   1. Write down three gifts you wish you had.
   2. Make a list of your friends or associates who possess those gifts.
   3. Call one of those people and ask for help in one of those areas.

Chapter 2

Treasure Chest—You

Every person is like a treasure chest housing many jewels and riches. Every jewel is a precious stone—a gift from God. God carefully selected and wrapped those gifts with the intent for us to use them to glorify Him and pursue our calling. In order for us to find out what those gifts are, to open up the treasure chest, we must first open our hearts to God. With His light, we can see inside the chest and discover the jewels. Then we take them out to assess if we can use them right away, gaze at their beauty, or determine if we'll need to clean them, polish them, and make them ready to use at a later time.

Some stones in their raw state take longer to be polished and ready for use. We need to be patient polishing those stones and wait until they become smooth and shiny. The same happens with our gifts. Some are discovered in their raw state, and patience is key. If we start using our gifts before they are ready, we will misuse or waste them. In contrast, there are gifts that take little time in the polishing stage. Yet others only need a little dusting before we can put them to use. Regardless of how long it takes for each gift to be ready, enjoying the process of discovering, assessing, cleaning, polishing, and ultimately using these gifts is fulfilling.

I started using the gift of writing ten years ago when I wrote my first book. I never thought I had that gift until I felt the urge to share with others all that I had inside. I told my husband that I felt as if I was going to explode if I didn't share my ideas and tips with working women so they could have a better chance at balancing their lives.

He suggested, "Why don't you write a devotional?" and that was it. I started writing the next day, and I don't think I'll ever stop. Now I write a blog each week, I wrote this book, and I'm a contributing writer to a newspaper. I discovered the gift, polished it, and I'm now using it continually with the intention of blessing others. This gift has helped me tremendously in business communications and as I write strategic plans for clients. God multiplies the use of each gift.

Once we polish each stone or gift, we can then display it for the world to see and enjoy. Gemstones have the capacity to allow the light to shine through, like emeralds, or to reflect the light, like pearls. The same happens with our gifts. Allowing God's light to shine through or reflect His light on our gifts, so others can be blessed, is a gift in itself.

Our gifts are for us and others to enjoy and for God to get the glory. Each gift has a special purpose. Our hearts can choose to use our gifts for others instead of for ourselves. We can act without having a hidden agenda, or becoming prideful. By keeping our motives pure, our gifts will also remain pure and be used to glorify God.

What does it mean to polish a gift? The dictionary defines the word "polish" as making smooth and glossy by rubbing or friction. It can also mean becoming refined or elegant as a person. The purpose of polishing something is to end up with a beautiful product, something we can use and be proud of. Our gifts, like precious stones, may not look so beautiful when they are found in the raw rock stage. Therefore, we need to do some work with each rock so we can end up with a usable gift. By rubbing or applying friction, a stone becomes smooth and shiny. The same happens when we apply friction to our gifts.

We apply friction in many ways. For example, as a writer and author, I need an editor. The first time I got my first book back edited, I thought I was going to cry. I felt like giving up. I thought I must be a terrible writer. But then I thought, *If I don't work on the editor's recommendations and make the changes, I will never improve as a writer*—especially since English is my second language. Polishing a book after seeing the editor's notes is very challenging, but it's a worthwhile exercise (the friction) in order to become better and produce an excellent product.

If you have a gift in the area of sports, you will need to be consistently diligent, practice, and work out hard to improve. If you, as an athlete, don't play often, either alone or with a team, you will not be able to play successfully. It takes effort, discipline, and commitment to be successful at any sport.

In the workplace, if you have the gift of leadership, you still need to train in that area by attending seminars, study on your own time to improve as a leader, and seek God for daily guidance. You may also want to look for additional opportunities to lead people, whether that would be at your church, community, or in the office. When I was working for a bank at the beginning of my career, I volunteered to lead a non-profit association as the local president. At the same time, I took self-study courses in a Management Certificate Program. Both experiences helped me become a better leader.

9

I imagine that from God's perspective, the world itself is a treasure chest that represents Jesus's inheritance. Every one of us is a jewel, a precious stone. God applies friction to us during our lifetime by taking us in His hands, cleansing us, polishing us, and making us ready to be used. Even though God is capable of using us whether we are ready or not, it is likely to be more enjoyable for us if we actually participate in the preparation. He enjoys the process of discovering us, loves us through the polishing, and is blessed when He uses us.

I am an impatient person, so God always takes opportunities to help me in that area. How? By making me wait! I have to wait for almost everything I want until it's His timing. The fact that I'm still waiting for things tells me He's not done training me! I wish I would learn quicker.

As individuals, we are gifts to each other. Just as some stones take longer to be polished, some of us take longer to be fully used by God. All of us living together with others in the treasure chest of this world help to polish each other in the rock tumbler of life.

As you discover every gift given to you by God, consider watching for the purpose of each gift to ensure you are using your gifts in your work. With gifts comes responsibility. God entrusts you with each one of those gifts and trusts you to use them for His glory by helping others.

Every gift and talent God gives you has a purpose in your life and in the lives of those around you. In my case, I have the gift of encouragement, so I use it every day to encourage someone. You just never know when *one* word will lift up a person that day. One word might be the message that person needed to hear at that moment.

1 Peter 4:10 (NLT) *God has given gifts to each of you from his great variety of spiritual gifts. Manage them well so that God's generosity can flow through you.*

- **Questions to ponder**

  1. How have you opened your heart to God's light so He can show you all the gifts He entrusted you with?
  2. How are you developing some of your gifts in your current job?
  3. If you have a polished gift, are you ready to use it for God's purpose?

- **Action items**

  1. Make a list of the gifts God entrusted with you.
  2. Make a list of the precious stones you are in the process of polishing.
  3. Display and use the gifts that are ready for others to enjoy. For example, display compassion toward others by serving at a food shelf once in a while. Use your wisdom to give good advice to a friend when they seek you out or ask you questions.

Chapter 3

What Kind of Tree
Would You Be?

God created everything. In this chapter I'm using a tree analogy to demonstrate the great variety of types of people God created. If you could see yourself as a tree, what kind would you choose to be? You may imagine yourself as the strong, tall, thick-trunk type of tree with beautiful branches and green, healthy leaves, a majestic-looking tree. But are you? Even big strong trees started out as little seeds, seeds that needed nourishment, the appropriate environment to grow in, and the care of the Master to care for them. Those trees needed the right soil to develop and grow strong roots.

Some trees are hollow and empty inside. When storms come, they fold like a little twig and break in two. What made them weak to begin with? What makes one tree really strong and another one weak? Was the soil missing some key nutrients as they were growing up, or was it the way they grew? Were the roots not strong enough to support their grown-up trunks? Other trees seem to withstand whatever type of storm comes their way. The storms pass and there they are, still standing. They may lose some branches, but they recover the next season and grow again.

What makes one person strong and another weak inside? Just like trees, some people grow up in an unhealthy environment and grow empty inside. On the outside, they look majestic and self-confident; but on the inside, they are dying. They are dried up. They have no life in them. Their roots are short and weak, which is why they cannot support the mature trunk. The soil, which is the heart, lacked love—a basic nutrient to grow up healthy.

As you grew up, there were people in your life who took the time to teach you, straighten you, and give you advice so you would grow up tall and strong. Others may not have had that person in their lives. I was blessed to have parents who taught me the ways of God early on and also disciplined me a lot (probably more than my siblings ... but probably with reason, I'm sure).

God created each kind of human being. Just as there are many types of trees (colors, sizes, and some that grow in different climates and terrains), so there are many kinds of people. Even within the same types of trees, they are each different. The same way, God created every person to be unique. Yet He created us all in His image. How can that be? Are we the same but at the same time different?

We are created in His image, meaning we all are spirit beings first that live in a physical body. The inside of each individual, the spirit, is unique. The outside of each person, the physical body, is also unique, with its own DNA. But we are all the same from His perspective because we are all children of God alike. He loves us all the same.

God is a creator, an inventor. He doesn't create the same thing repeatedly. Inventors like to create new things. They come up with new ideas all the time. Because we are created in His image, we inherited these characteristics as well. We would get bored without variety. Some people are more gifted than others in this area.

God created all nature with one common purpose, which is to give Him glory. God created humans with many purposes and to give Him glory is one of them as well. He also gave each person a unique purpose and equipped us with unique gifts.

We become the person God intended us to be depending on several factors. Is the soil of your heart soft and ready to receive His Word, or is it hardened by the experiences in life and you are not able to receive the seed of His Word? Are you watering the soil of your heart enough when you receive a new seed or Word from God? Are you supplying enough water to your roots so they grow strong and deeper in the things of God by reading His Word often? Are you getting sufficient sun, the light of God, to illuminate you and work with the water to help you grow in Him? Or are you sitting in the dark where you can't see what God wants of you?

Trees live outside in the open, exposed to nature. People live in a world that exposes us to the winds, rain, and storms of life. Therefore, we need deep roots; our beliefs need to be rooted in God's Word in order to survive the storms that come at us, sometimes on a daily basis. God is our stronghold, our safety place, and our hope. This is where God created us different from trees. He created us in His image and, therefore, He takes care of us in a way that goes beyond the way He cares for the rest of His creation.

In nature, some trees may last longer than humans, but they can also be gone in one single storm. They can be uprooted and die. They become dust and disintegrate into the ground. The same way, your body will eventually disintegrate. But you are an eternal being. Even though your life here on earth is nothing but vapor compared to eternity, your life matters. What you do here on earth, the decisions you make here on a daily basis affect the rest of your life here and in eternity.

We may be like trees in many aspects, and it is fun to compare ourselves to such beautiful creations of God, but we were created for bigger purposes. We are important to God in every way and for eternity. He has a supernatural plan for each one of us. He has a unique plan for *you*.

Life here is short and we need to be aware of that reality at all times. With this revelation in our hearts, we can act and do the things God calls us to do. One of those things we are called to do is to work—and we can find purpose in our work every day of our lives. Then we will be in His will and be able to fulfill His calling and plans in our lives.

If I compare myself to a tree, sometimes when everything is going well, I feel I could be an oak tree. I feel strong. I can stand tall and feel almost invincible. Other times, when a close relationship is not going well, or like when I left my job to start a new business, I have felt like a lonely, lost tree, exposed in the wilderness with no protection against the storms. I felt vulnerable and weak.

Other times, like after the war in Nicaragua, my country of origin which my family left in 1979 during the revolution to live in the Dominican Republic, or after surviving a hurricane when I was living in Dominican Republic, I felt like lightning just hit me. My life as I knew it changed forever. I felt burnt and broken. That feeling is similar to feeling burnt out from working too much. When my children were little and I was working full-time, and my husband was going to school and working full-time, too, I eventually felt weak, burnt out, and tired. But throughout all of these circumstances, God has been there.

When I felt like an oak tree, God was there to shine on me and provide shelter and shade to others through me. When I felt like the lonely tree out in the open, He provided nourishment and made me feel strong again. When I felt broken and burnt, He provided sun, rain, and sent other trees around me to bring me back to life. God cared for me every time. He cares for you, too, no matter what kind of tree you may feel like being right now in your life.

MATTHEW 7:11 (NLT) *So if you sinful people know how to give good gifts to your children, how much more will your heavenly Father give good gifts to those who ask him.*

• QUESTIONS TO PONDER

1. What are you doing now to prepare for eternity?
2. What things do you like about the person God created you to be?
3. If there are things you don't like about your life right now, what are you doing to change those things?

- **ACTION ITEMS**

  1. Get to know yourself and start loving the person that God created you to be.
  2. Get to know your Creator by spending time with Him in prayer.
  3. Ask God to help you create an environment where you can flourish and be the beautiful person He made you to be.

Chapter 4

Apply Your Natural Gifts to Succeed in Your Career

We are all born with natural gifts and talents. These are the things that are easy for us to do, that come naturally, and the ones other people usually notice that we do well. Taking these gifts for granted can be a great mistake. We need to find out what these gifts are and develop them so we can use them for the Kingdom of God. We will then be fulfilled.

The first step in determining what things we like to do is by knowing ourselves well. Many people go through life, work at many jobs, and never really stop to think about the things they really enjoy or like doing. Each person is a unique individual with strengths and weaknesses, gifted in some areas and not gifted in others. God carefully planned what gifts to give to each one of us.

Knowing what we like and don't like, and knowing what we are good at and what we are not good at, are revelations we need to have in our hearts. We need to determine the difference between activities we are good at but we don't enjoy doing and the activities we are good at and *do* enjoy.

When you have that knowledge about yourself, you can choose a job and career that involves doing what you love, and your chances of succeeding are much higher. Sometimes, however, due to circumstances in your life, you may end up in a job you don't like or are not as interested in pursuing long term. In those situations, remember God is in control, and He knows why you are there. If you are in this situation, make a list of the positives and negatives of your job. Also make a list of the skills you could acquire while you are there that might help you in your future career goals. I strongly believe that everybody can learn something new in each job—even a boring job. Take advantage of the situation and acquire new skills and expertise that will make you a better person or even a better candidate for a job you'd like more.

I have had many jobs, and I have loved most of them. When I was thirty years old, I was asked to manage a bank branch. I was excited to become a manager and extremely grateful for the opportunity, because I had never supervised employees before. But when I started the job, I realized it was not what I wanted. It was probably the hardest job I had in my banking career. Why? Thinking back, there were many factors that contributed to my disappointment. One was that the branch didn't have a manager for the previous three months, and I had no one to train me. I came to an empty desk! Another factor was that the current employees had relationship issues that I had to resolve immediately. A third factor that contributed to making this job difficult was being the only woman among thirty other branch managers. I felt alone.

Even though this was a hard job, I am thankful for that experience, because I gained significant management and general banking experience, which helped me later to start a bank from scratch. I learned very quickly how to resolve employee issues and how to manage difficult situations with clients. In addition, I gained a lot of lending and budgeting knowledge, which also helped me later. God never wastes anything!

Some people are not motivated to move up the ladder at work. They don't want the stress that comes with greater responsibility. Not everybody is cut out to be a manager, and others simply don't want to be responsible for anyone but themselves. Some workers just want to punch in and out and forget about work for the rest of the day. They may not be interested in the overall good of their company or even what products they sell or produce. They just want a paycheck, to survive, and pay the bills. They want no worries or additional responsibilities of any kind.

That is okay, too. But it is not okay to go to work purposeless! Find a purpose in that job, or you will become bored, unmotivated, and eventually bitter about your work. It is satisfying to do the same job for many years when you have a purpose.

I was at my last job for ten years. That's a long time to be at the same job—especially because I'm a people person, and my role was all "behind the scenes" with no client contact. However, I had a purpose from the start—to help fulfill my boss's dream to start his own bank, to grow the bank with a strong infrastructure, and to learn to run a bank as a business. If I hadn't had that job for those ten years, I would not be able to later start my own business to help other banks be successful. In addition, God gave me several opportunities to continue to learn and grow within the same job. I was promoted four times and grew a staff from one to eight to help me manage all the operations of the bank. I learned to run a bank as a business and helped create an infrastructure to support the bank's growth from zero to more than 300 million dollars in assets.

Regardless of what we do for a living, what matters most is *why* we do what we do. It matters that we do our work from our hearts and with purpose. We need to let God show us His purpose for us being in a particular job at a specific time in our lives. Maybe the purpose is to be the light in your workplace. The Bible says in Matthew 5:13 (NLT), "You are the salt of the earth. But what good is salt if it has lost its flavor? Can you make it salty again? It will be thrown out and trampled underfoot as worthless." You may be the only person who knows Christ, and He needs you to be the "salt" in that office or field. Sometimes you don't know, and may never know, why He has you at a place. In those situations, work in faith, knowing He has the best plans for your life.

Find your purpose in every job. Find the purpose of your company. Why does your company do what it does? If you don't know, ask your manager. What motivated the founder of the company to start this company? Usually, the person who started the company or business had a good idea and good intentions. Work for a company where you can align your beliefs and core values with the company's mission and core values so you can work for a common purpose. For example, if you love the medical field and you chose the career of nursing because you wanted to help people feel better, then choose a clinic or hospital where you can feel you are helping your patients, where you can love on them and serve them while they recover. If you are working for a hospital that only cares about profits, wants to speed up patient care, and doesn't allow you time to connect with patients, you might not be working in the right place for you to use your gifts and work purposefully. My brother, who is a pulmonologist, partnered with a clinic and hospital where he can fulfill his calling to help people feel better and be restored to health.

Finding purpose in every job we have is crucial for our success in life. When we are purposeless, we become disgruntled with the world, and it shows. Usually, our family suffers first, next our friends get tired of hearing us complain, and eventually nobody wants to be around us. Because work occupies a big part of our daily lives, it is important to find the reason to get up in the morning other than just to pay bills and survive.

ROMANS 11:29 (NLT) *For God's gifts and his call can never be withdrawn.*

- **QUESTIONS TO PONDER**

    1. How well do you know *you?*
    2. What activities do you *love* doing? These may be some of your gifts.
    3. What activities do you dislike doing? These may give you an idea of areas you are not gifted at.

- **ACTION ITEMS**
  1. List three examples of things that cause you stress.
  2. List three examples of things or activities that help you relax.
  3. Picture an environment that gives you peace, and try to create that atmosphere at home somewhere. For example, if you're like me and love the ocean, buy pictures of the ocean and put them in a place where you can look often. You can also buy CDs with the sound of the ocean. If you like skiing, vacation in places where you can ski, or hang pictures of the mountains on your walls.

Chapter 5

Music Within You

If we were to compare ourselves to a musical instrument, we could say we have the ability to create our own music. We could create our own songs, unique and individual. Part of leaving a legacy in this earth is to leave behind the songs we made with our lives. Just as songs remind people of places, friends, or seasons in their lives, the songs of our lives will remind people of us—the lives we lived.

Every day we live, we write notes on the music sheet, creating our own song one note at a time. At birth, our music sheet is blank, ready to start being used, ready to be written upon. Our last breath here on earth may be the last note written on our music sheet. What style of songs we write depends entirely on what kind of life we choose to live. Just as there are many genres of music such as rock, blues, country, pop, classical, and others, there are many kinds of songs we could create throughout our lives.

Sometimes things happen that may make us change the speed of our songs. Maybe we need to slow the song down or speed it up. Maybe we need to include some higher notes by taking new risks. Or maybe we need to lower the tune to mellow down when we have been living on high stress, high pitch for a while. When we share our life story with others through words or actions, we are playing our songs to people.

The lifestyle we choose to live will influence our songs tremendously. The choices we make on a daily basis about the work we do, how hard we work in our jobs, the goals we have for our careers, how we treat our coworkers, and how much we help them, all play a part in our song writing.

God sees us all as a big orchestra that He put together. He is the conductor, the One we all need to follow in order to create the perfect arrangement. He is the Creator of the big masterpiece, the One who involves and includes every single person He created. There is a time and place of preparation where all the new musicians are practicing until they are ready to join the big orchestra and play in harmony with the rest. As time goes by, some musicians retire (when they die) and some new musicians are added (the ones ready to play in the orchestra).

One of the key components of a big orchestra is to have harmony amongst all the players. Without harmony, we have chaos and confusion. If there is no harmony, there is no order. God is an orderly God. He created everything with a specific order, harmony, and balance. Humans tend to create the opposite—disorder and chaos. Everybody wants to go on their own and create their own music, sometimes at the wrong times. Even though God gave us the freedom to create our own music, we still have to play with the rest of His creation and be in harmony. That's why God put boundaries in place for us to follow. That's why there are training camps for us to participate, and classes for us to learn music. The same way, there are some things we need to do in order to be good participants and contributors in the workplace.

In order for us to be successful in the workplace, wherever that may be, we need to prepare. From the time we go to elementary school, then high school, then college or trade school, we are preparing to join the workforce—regardless of the nature of the work—at home or elsewhere. We prepare to be good contributors to society. We all need to do what God called us to do during the various seasons in our lives. For those who take breaks from work outside the home to raise children, I recommend keeping your business and technical skills current in case you choose someday to go back to a career you previously found fulfilling.

Part of belonging to an orchestra is reading and playing music. Part of the preparation is to learn an instrument. Some of us will choose our voices as our instrument to play. Others will choose the piano, the clarinet, the flute, guitar, drums, or trombone. It doesn't matter which instrument we choose. What matters is that we find our purpose in playing that instrument and locate a place in the orchestra. God gave us different gifts, and those gifts help us choose the instruments to use in order to make a contribution to the big orchestra of life. God may sometimes ask us to play a different instrument for a season. We need to trust God when He puts us in those positions. All the unique instruments are needed in order to make a masterpiece. God wrote the ultimate song of life.

Just as the orchestra is arranged in groups by instruments (guitars are in one place, flutes are all together, and so on), so does God arrange us in groups of people where we can practice and learn together. Each team has a leader or teacher so the others can follow and cooperate with that person. The team's responsibility is to practice, work hard, and learn the music so they can participate in the orchestra when the time comes to play. Each one of us has to make the effort to get to know the other players, their styles of music, the instruments they play, and how we can support them. Our participation in these groups, which we can call our workplace, influences how we write our own song of life. How we interact with others can be helpful or disruptive to our own songwriting. Sometimes we may get stuck on a note that we don't know whether it belongs in our song. Other times we may not know if we should go higher in pitch or lower. It is similar with our lives. Sometimes we may need help from our friends in deciding whether to take a new job. Other times we may not know if the time is right to make changes. The change may bring more stress to our lives than we can handle at the time.

The important thing to remember is that we are all writing our songs every day of our lives. Every choice and decision we make will have an impact on our song. God puts people in our paths so we can help them write their songs and they can help us write ours. We are all here because God put us here, and He created the big Masterpiece. We all work for Him and we have a duty to fulfill our purpose in the orchestra of life, living in harmony and loving each other. God continues to show us how He created us each as unique, yet we are all equally important in His eyes. He gave us one common purpose in life, which is to bring people to His Kingdom and to love Him.

PSALM 13:6 (NLT) *I will sing to the Lord because he has been so good to me.*

- **QUESTIONS TO PONDER**

  1. Have you discovered the music in you?
  2. What style of music are you writing with your lifestyle?
  3. What song will play of your life when you're gone?

- **ACTION ITEMS**

  1. Recognize you are important to God, and He wants you to write a song with your life.
  2. Ask God to help you in writing your song by helping you make godly choices.
  3. Ask God how you can help others write their songs.

Chapter 6

Avoid Comparing Yourself to Others

Y ou are a unique creation of God with special gifts. By comparing yourself to others you are essentially telling God that He didn't do well enough with you, your self-esteem deteriorates, and you are not be able to grow personal or professionally.

We don't know why He gave some gifts to others and not to us. We don't know what His purposes are for every person. We only need to find out what our own purpose is, so we can use our gifts to accomplish our highest calling.

People who compare themselves to others can become insecure, indecisive, and eventually bitter. They continually second-guess what they do and what they say. With time, they lose track of who they really are. People who compare themselves to others can lose their own identity by acting and looking like someone else. They can become depressed to the point of hating themselves.

I imagine that from God's perspective, we may be hurting God by not loving ourselves. He is the Master of the Universe, and we are questioning what He does? How can we dare question Him? We admire other things such as grandiose mountains, beautiful skies, and great flowing rivers—nature in general. But sometimes we don't admire the enormous work it took to create a human being. Furthermore, we don't thank Him in the first place for creating us as unique individuals with the capacity to love Him and to live eternally with Him. How can we dare question His decisions about what gifts, looks, and talents He gives us and others? I assume that most of us have questioned God at some point in our lives. But I don't think it's a good idea. A better idea is to *trust* God.

I am purposed and fully committed to use every gift and talent God gave me because it is the least I can do to thank and honor Him. One of my prayers is to be able to use each gift He provided and to look for the opportunities that present themselves in my daily life.

There are some things we cannot use right at the moment, but God will let us know when it's time to use them. In the meantime, our responsibility is to train ourselves and prepare those gifts so they are ready to be used when that time comes. For instance, I know I have the gift for public speaking. It's taken me many years to have the opportunity to do that as much as I would like to. I've had to prepare myself to become a better speaker and wait for the right doors to open.

If you find you are comparing yourself to others, stop immediately. The more you make that comparison, the lower your self-esteem will go, and the harder it is to recover. Everybody compares themselves to somebody else at one point or another in their lives. Sometimes you might do it for fun, but those words of comparison can sink into your heart and create negative expectations of yourself. Those expectations can become reality and pretty soon you become what you believe of yourself. You are what you say you are.

Your mouth speaks what is in your heart. The more you say negative things about yourself, the more your ears hear it, and those words penetrate your soul.

I remember the years I hated my body. I assume most women go through a season in their lives when they don't like what they see in the mirror. I had to stop that behavior. Making that change took a lot of positive reinforcement, a lot of hard work, and finally accepting that this is the body God gave me. Now I do the best with what I have, and I'm happy with my body. It may not be perfect, but that's okay. It is perfect in the eyes of God.

There is hope. You have control over what you think and what you say. Ask God to help you by making you aware of negative thoughts and words you may say about yourself when you compare yourself to others. Change those negative words to positive words. Instead of saying, "I'm not as smart as that person," say, "Thank you, Father, for making me a smart person and for allowing me the chance to get an education."

There are things you can do in order to improve yourself in many areas. For example, if you are overweight, you probably have compared yourself to a thin person and said, "I wish I could be that thin." Well, you can be. Start exercising, and change your eating behaviors. In some cases, people gain weight due to medical reasons, but those are exceptions and not the common reason for being overweight. Nowadays, many people in America are overweight due to bad nutrition and lack of exercise. It is possible to lose weight but it takes determination, commitment, and resolution.

Exercise is an important part of every person's daily lifestyle. If you make working out a fun event, you will look forward to it instead of seeing it as a chore or painful activity.

Plenty of information is available about which diet is best and what exercise plan might be best for you. The bottom line for all of us is, as we grow older, we will need to eat less and exercise more—not fair but it is the reality.

Every time we strive to change a behavior, we have to put forth an effort if we are to succeed. But the change is worth the hard work. When we see the results, we get charged up, motivated, and encouraged to do even more and to change other areas of our lives for the better.

Some things we cannot change, such as our height, the color of our eyes, or our skin. For those things, we need to thank God for the way He made us. He chose the color of our skin, and we can embrace it as part of who we are. I think He likes variety. And even though He made each of us to be unique and different, we are all equally important in the eyes of God. He made us all with the same love, and He sent His Son Jesus to die for each one of us *individually*. We are each a child of God.

The moment we stop comparing ourselves to other people, we allow God to start working in our lives, and we start growing in every area of our lives. We allow Him to reveal hidden gifts we didn't know we had; and as we develop and use those gifts, He gives us new ones. He wants to bless us so much, and we don't let Him if we are preoccupied comparing ourselves to others and coveting what we don't have. God has an abundant supply of gifts, and He is just waiting for us to ask Him for them. Sometimes He gives us new gifts to bless us, because He knows we will use them for His glory.

God sees our hearts. He knows when we want a new talent or gift to use it for ourselves and when we want it to further His kingdom. We cannot fool God, because He knows what we think. Remember that when we don't use certain gifts He gave us, God may take those gifts away and give them to somebody else who will use them. For example, if He gave us the gift of leadership but we don't want to step up and take leadership roles—whether they are at work or as a volunteer—He will close doors of opportunities and others will be chosen to do those tasks. The process works in a simple way: He gives us the gifts; we develop them and make them ready to be used. He opens doors for us and we step through those doors in faith in order to use those gifts.

Examples of natural gifts include singing, composing music, creating beautiful art, or an aptitude for engineering, math, or chemistry. Examples of spiritual gifts are prophesy, wisdom, knowledge, teaching, serving, giving, praying, encouraging, and many others.

Because there are so many natural and spiritual gifts, there are many ways we might compare ourselves to others. Some people compare the natural gifts they have, their physical bodies, or their material possessions. Others compare themselves spiritually to others, and that is dangerous territory. Spiritual gifts are the most important gifts we possess, because they are eternal. When we die, who cares how tall we were, how much money we had, or how well we could sing? But if we start using the spiritual gifts here on earth, we can use them for an eternity with God. The gifts I'm talking about are the true riches of heaven. Besides the spiritual gifts listed above, God gave specific spiritual gifts to the church: the apostles, the prophets, the evangelists, the pastors, and teachers (Ephesians 4:11 NLT). These are gifts that carry serious responsibility and those that are charged with them will answer to God someday.

ROMANS 12:6-8 (NLT), *God has given each of us the ability to do certain things well. So if God has given you the ability to prophesy, speak out when you have faith that God is speaking through you. If your gift is that of serving others, serve them well. If you are a teacher, do a good job of teaching. If your gift is to encourage others, do it! If you have money, share it generously. If God has given you leadership ability, take the responsibility seriously. And if you have a gift for showing kindness to others, do it gladly.*

- **QUESTIONS TO PONDER**

  1. In what ways have you compared yourself to other people?
  2. How did comparing yourself to others make you feel?
  3. If comparing yourself to others is a common behavior for you, how can you start changing that pattern today?

- **ACTION ITEMS**

  1. Stop comparing yourself to others today.
  2. Start thanking God for every gift and talent He gave you. Make a list.
  3. Begin sharing your gifts with others by using your gifts to serve people.

Chapter 7

What's in Your Heart?

The heart—what a complex concept to grasp. The physical heart is the core of the human body. It is the mechanism, or organ, that pumps blood—life—to the rest of the body. Our physical hearts are crucial to our life and survival. They are the center of our being. Our spiritual hearts do the same function for our spirit. The spiritual heart holds the core of our beliefs. Our heart is where our values and ethical standards reside. Our hearts are the soil where the Word of God is planted and where the seed of His Word grows. What's in our hearts spills into the rest of our bodies and comes out on the surface. Therefore, it is extremely important to store the right moral principles in our hearts with the Word of God as our foundation.

When we hear the Word of God (the seed) for the first time, that Word is planted in our soil, our hearts. It is up to us to make sure that seed doesn't wither and die, because the Bible says in Matthew 13:19 (NLT) that as soon as the seed is planted, the enemy comes to steal it and destroy it. We have to guard that seed by watering it with more Word, by hearing it again and again until it sinks into our hearts, until it starts growing roots. The Word of God, that seed, can wither at any time, however. Even when we have taken care of the seed and watered it for a long time, even when the seed grows roots and grows into a full-blown plant, if at that time, we stop watering it, it can die.

The word "heart" has been overused and the meaning is misunderstood. We shouldn't speak lightly about the matters of the heart. We have to be careful when saying or using expressions such as "his heart is for us to do ..." or "I know his heart or her heart." We need to be careful not to misrepresent people's hearts. Most importantly, we must be careful not to misrepresent God's heart. We only get to know other people's hearts by spending time with them, talking with them, and having heart-to-heart conversations. When we build relationships based on trust, we can start getting to know the other person's heart. The same way, we can only get to know God's heart by spending time with Him in prayer, reading His Word, and meditating in it. When we spend time with God, we learn to trust Him, and He starts pouring His heart into ours. When we have a revelation in our hearts of the heart of God, we can start representing Him well on this earth.

In the workplace, we may be given a written job description that lists our job functions, our responsibilities, who we report to, and what the expectations of us are in that particular position. To be successful at our job, we need to know what our job description is to know what is expected of us. It is also important that we get to know our boss. It is important to learn how the boss likes to communicate and how the boss wants us to do our jobs. Being open to his or her advice and input in our work, and learning more about the boss as an individual will also help us to have a successful relationship.

In our spiritual lives, part of being a child of God is being His worker as well. When we are His workers, we have a job description. We cannot do that job well unless we know the heart of our boss. We need to know what He expects of us, how He wants us to do the job, and what our responsibilities are. He also wants us to learn more about Him.

But have you ever asked yourself the question, "What is in *my* heart?" I am hopeful that, in addition to having your beliefs and ethical standards in your heart, you also have desires in your heart that you want to fulfill at some point in your life. Knowing what those desires are and recognizing God put them in your heart is crucial to you finding the purpose and calling in your life and in every job you do. Find purpose in your work; do not just work to have a job and earn a living. Find the purpose in whatever job you're in; otherwise, you will get bored and lose your motivation. When you find your purpose in your job, you will have a fire that comes from your heart. That fire is what propels you to do well and to work hard, because you know you are there for a reason. God put you there for a purpose. You have a mission to accomplish.

God put desires in your heart for your life, but He also placed the desire for you to help others along the way. One common purpose we all have is to help each other. We just have to find our niche. Just as companies focus on a specific target market (niche), we need to focus our desire to help others in a specific area or group of people. We can't help everyone in the entire world, because we have limited time and resources. What group of people do you want to help? It can be the people at work, the elderly, or orphan children. It doesn't matter. God needs people to help in every area. There are plenty of organizations that are established with the purpose and mission of helping others.

God is the One who puts desires in our hearts. But the most important thing that we need to put in our hearts in order to be successful in this world is Jesus. He is our Lord and Savior who gave it all up for us so we can spend eternity with Him in heaven. Without having Jesus in our hearts, we cannot do anything worthwhile, and we will never find our true purpose for why we are here to begin with. We won't find purpose in any job or any work we do. When we find Jesus and invite Him in our hearts, then we find everlasting life and everything that comes with it.

If you don't have Jesus in your heart, today is your day! Simply invite Him in and ask Him for forgiveness. He's been waiting for you to invite Him all your life. If you already have Him in your heart, live for Him, dedicate your work to Him.

When I ask myself the very personal question, what's in *my* heart? I am overwhelmed by a desire to love and help people. When I asked myself, "Which people?" the answer became clear in my heart: my niche is to help working people. They are the ones I feel qualified and equipped to help based on my own work experience and my gifts.

I also find in my heart the desire to help working people in poor countries. In December 2012 I had the opportunity to go back to Nicaragua with Opportunity International, a nonprofit organization that works with the poor in about twenty-eight countries around the world by providing them micro loans. Over 85 percent of their clients are women and their average payback ratio is over 95 percent. My heart was overwhelmed with compassion for the poor working women we visited. These are women who are hard workers, full of energy, creativity, and who have a desire to succeed. God showed me in that trip that these are full-time working moms just like I've been all these years. I simply had greater opportunities and the immense blessing of living in America. Opportunity International is now one of the organizations I support because they are in my heart. Their mission aligns with my mission.

ROMANS 10:9-10 (NLT) *For if you confess with your mouth that Jesus is Lord and believe in your heart that God raised him from the dead, you will be saved. For it is by believing in your heart that you are made right with God, and it is by confessing with your mouth that you are saved.*

- QUESTIONS TO PONDER

    1. Is Jesus in your heart? If not, invite Him into your heart today.
    2. What are the desires of your heart?
    3. What do you desire to do for other people?

- ACTION ITEMS

    1. Stay connected to God's heart by praying often.
    2. God Himself put desires in your heart. Write them down and start acting on them.
    3. Start doing something for someone else today.

Chapter 8

Discover Your Own Path to Success

In the big picture of life there is only one path that leads to real *life*. That is the narrow path of walking with Jesus Christ.

Each person defines success in a different way. Success for one person may be having a lot of material possessions, owning a company, and having several children. For others, it may be simply that they found Christ in their lives, can pay the monthly bills, are healthy, and live a low-stress lifestyle. Yet for others, like the poor women I visited from Nicaragua, success to them was simply to feed and clothe their children and ensure they obtained an education. It doesn't matter how you define success. What matters is that you attain success during this life—the success you desire.

Regardless of how you define success in your life, there is a cost to obtain it. You need to find out what the cost for your success will be before you start on that path. Sometimes we think, for example, we want to be a doctor because doctors make a lot of money. Well, are you willing to go to school for twelve years of your life and not see your family very often? Are you willing to wait to get married and have children until you finish school? The answers to these questions may be overwhelming. But don't be discouraged, if you want to become a doctor, there are many ways you can do it.

The same applies if you want to be an entrepreneur. There is a cost to owning your own business—both financially as well as time. Many people lose their home and sacrifice valuable possessions in order to get their business off the ground. Are you willing to move to a different home for the sake of the business? Are you willing to work endless hours at the beginning when you can't afford to pay for an employee to help you with the administration of the company? There are two main points here. The first point is that, with every success story, there is a cost and a price you need to pay. The second point is that you need to know what the costs are, and then make the decision to start the business.

When defining your own success, be careful to avoid choosing somebody else's success that could lead you to follow somebody else's path. Ask yourself many questions in order to ensure you choose the right road on which you will walk for a long time. Be willing to change course if necessary and to go back to the starting point if things don't work out the way you expected. Be willing to take risks and follow through. Have a strong faith in God and know you are following your success road according to His will, not yours.

In order for you to walk successfully on your own path to success, you may need to make many changes along the way. For example, if you want to become a manager at a company, you may have to start by leading a small group project. You will need to learn to be patient and wait until the right opportunity presents itself for a bigger leadership role. You may also have to attend classes to educate yourself and become a good manager. If you are not used to dealing with people and are not a team-oriented type of person, you may have to change your behavior, work in teams first under someone else's leadership so you can lead one later.

Sometimes your path may be diverted by circumstances out of your control. For example, you finally get the job you have been waiting for and, all of a sudden, the company is sold. Now you are faced with the possibility of losing your new job, and you panic. How do you handle those changes? In this situation, you may have to create a new opportunity for yourself in the new company or negotiate a new deal or compete for your same position if it's a duplicate.

Just as road builders run into circumstances and challenges out of their control, we all do, too, in life. In such cases, are you equipped to build a bridge if you need one between the two companies? An example of building a bridge may be to establish relationships with the leadership of the new company early in the process so they get to know you. If you end up losing your job, are you ready to jump with a parachute if you have to? Is your landing gear ready? An example of a parachute could be to establish an employment agreement prior to your company ever selling, just in case and also depending on the position you hold in your company. Your landing gear can be anything from the severance pay you would receive to your personal plans for what you will do with your time once you are unemployed.

If you are like most people, you don't like to think about these situations. We all need to be smart and plan ahead, always believing God will take care of you in the end. Part of your landing gear has to be the Word of God, knowing that no matter where you land, God will be there with you.

He will help you build bridges and put on your parachute, if needed.

Sometimes you may get lost and disoriented during the journey. Life is not an easy ride for anybody, and that's why you need people to help you along the way. When you find yourself with no job, do you have people around you to keep you on track and accountable? Do you have people you trust to whom you can ask for directions? The people God puts in your path are there for a purpose and you will need to, at some point in your life, swallow your pride and ask for help. Sometimes we think we are supposed to live this life on our own, and we forget God did not intend for us to do it that way.

During the course of your life, you will probably fall many times. It is in those times when you can reach out and ask for help from the people He surrounds you with. Most importantly, do you have God to guide you on a daily basis, to light your path, to hold your hand, and to pick you up when you fall?

PROVERBS 3:5-6 (NLT) *Trust in the Lord with all your heart; do not depend on your own understanding. Seek his will in all you do, and he will direct your paths.*

- **QUESTIONS TO PONDER**

  1. How do you define success for your own life? Whose success path are you on—yours or someone else's and how did you get on it?
  2. What is the cost to be on your path? How are you willing to pay the price for your success?
  3. What do you need to do or change in your life to get on the the path you choose?

- **ACTION ITEMS**

  1. Choose your own pathway to success.
  2. Equip yourself by being prepared to make changes, by having the people around you to help you, and by having a relationship with God.
  3. Educate yourself and learn the cost of your success. Then make a decision and go for it.

Chapter 9

Climb Your Own Mountain

I had the opportunity to attend a conference in Phoenix, Arizona. The hotel was right by Camelback Mountain. I went with my boss and one of our bank directors, a retired business entrepreneur. On the second day, my boss said to us, "Let's skip tomorrow afternoon sessions and let's go climb Camelback Mountain."

I immediately said yes, and the next day we went on our adventure.

To climb a mountain can take months of preparation to be physically fit to endure the hike. You need some tools and equipment to make it to the top. The only reason I was confident I could climb the mountain is because I had been working out a lot harder in the previous year than I ever had before. I know this was a little mountain—only 1.2 miles up—but it was my first mountain. I was very excited to make the climb.

Part of being prepared was to have the right clothing. My boss and I both had workout clothes. Our friend had tennis shoes but no workout clothes. He also had an issue with his knee, so after the first five minutes into the trip, our friend decided to go to the side and enjoy the view and the restful time. He encouraged us to continue the journey without him. I had also brought a bottle of water, but my boss had to carry it for me in his shorts' pocket because I needed both hands to climb up. He didn't bring water, which he regretted later.

As we continued to climb up the one- and two-feet high rocks, we started to sweat and needed the water. But guess what? I was the only one with the water bottle. No matter how many times I offered to share my water, my boss said no, that he was fine. At one point, he was lightheaded and told me to say good-bye to his wife and kids for him (kiddingly).

Several times he wanted to go back because he felt bad that our friend was alone waiting for us at the bottom of the mountain. I gave him a hard time and told him, "Are you using that as an excuse so you can stop and go back?" Before he had time to respond, I said, "No way, we're climbing up and are going all the way up to the top!" And we did.

We stopped a couple of times to enjoy the view (and catch our breath). When we finally made it to the top, we had a 360-degree view of the city. It was an amazing and unforgettable experience. When it was time to come down— the descent was scarier than going up. If I missed a step, I was going down! When we reached the bottom, I felt a huge sense of accomplishment that I've never felt before.

So here is what I learned from this experience:

During our lives we will have a mountain or mountains to climb, and we need to be ready when the moment comes. These mountains are the job opportunities that come our way, struggles we encounter, and experiences we live through during the course of our lives. God will open up opportunities for each of us, and we need to be ready to jump with both feet and take the step in faith.

The preparation needed is threefold: physical, mental, and spiritual. If you follow the analogy of climbing the mountain, physically you need to be in good cardio shape so you can climb. It takes a lot of effort and training to go up and actually make it to the top. Right there on Camelback they told us that, on average, three people die per year—one of a heart attack and two others get off the trail and fall off a cliff. Part of the physical preparation you need is to acquire knowledge, which starts in school. Formal education is key to succeed in the business world.

You will also need to study the mountain you decide to climb. Learn what the dangers are, what the opportunities are, and the challenges you may encounter. You need to do your homework. Then you will need to create a plan and follow it, but be flexible for unforeseen circumstances that will require a change in course. However, don't get so off course that you lose sight of where you were going in the first place and end up falling off a cliff. Get used to asking yourself the questions, *Why am I here? What does God want me to learn from this situation (good or bad)? What am I afraid of? Am I having fun?* Being aware of your circumstances can help you make decisions down the road or even save your life.

You need to prepare and train yourself mentally to stay focused, dedicated, and disciplined enough to not quit. You need to be prepared to make tough decisions when you are presented with more than one way to climb the mountain but both are difficult. You need to be okay when one of your friends is left behind. You need to accept the fact that not everyone will make it to the top. Many will choose to go back. Others will simply stop at a certain level and stay there. Yet others will follow you to the top and be right there with you. You need to know if you are ready and willing to take the responsibility to lead the team, which means you need additional training and strength. You also need to be okay following others. During the journey, you may start following the leader, but during the hike, he or she may turn the leadership to you for whatever reason. You need to be ready to help others, share your resources, and help coworkers when they are tired and need a hand to climb over that hard spot.

When you follow, make sure you follow by choice. Look where your leader is going, make an assessment of his or her route and then choose to follow him or her. Sometimes you may choose to go another route that will get you to your goal as well but was easier for you. Sometimes you will make a mistake and what you thought was best turned out to be worst. Be ready in those times to admit you made a mistake and apologize, if necessary. Share what you learned with others who come after you.

During your working life you will likely work with the four generations: Traditionalists, Baby Boomers, Generation X, and Millennials or Gen Y. Some of your coworkers will be from the Traditionalist generation who already climbed their mountain and will be happy to stay at the bottom and watch you go up your own mountain. They will mentor you, cheer you up, and encourage you to finish your journey. Respect them, ask them questions, and learn all you can from them. They want to help you succeed. Don't see them as an obstacle but as an opportunity to learn and grow.

You will also work with Baby Boomers who are probably the ones at the top of the mountain right now and are thinking on how to get down without hurting themselves. They can also help you get to the top and will provide you

~~with opportunities to take over their leadership. You will be~~ climbing your mountain with Generation X coworkers who will work hard alongside you. Gen X coworkers have great opportunities to work together and climb even higher than their Baby Boomer colleagues. If you are a Gen X, then you can help those behind you, the Gen Y's, and you can also help the Baby Boomers reach their goals to get to the top or start their descent, depending on their situation.

Lastly, you will also work with the younger generation or Gen Y. They will help you with new ideas and can teach you new technologies that you have not used in the past. If you are a Gen Y, then you have a lot of opportunities to climb up your mountain. Don't be afraid to ask for help and learn from all the other generations that went before you. Earn their respect by working hard and being humble, knowing you have a lot to learn from them.

We cannot forget that most of the time, no matter how long we stay at the top of the mountain, at some point, we will come down. I envision that in a couple of ways: There may be smaller mountains we will need to climb early in our careers, and they will be preparation for bigger mountains, larger assignments that God has in store for us. We'll need to come down the smaller mountains and embark in the journey to climb the bigger mountain. Then we will have the experience and knowledge to conquer larger mountains. We will be more careful to not make the same mistakes and will do some things differently. There will be the time to step down and let the younger generation take over. We need to take the time to mentor them and teach them what we've learned without feeling threatened. We need to enjoy the journey coming down, enjoy the views, and know that at the bottom lies rest and the satisfaction of knowing we accomplished much in our lives. We finished our race.

Spiritually, the journey starts with an open heart to God, allowing Him to fill us up with his Holy Spirit and wisdom. Spiritual training means we spend time with God, just in His presence, enjoying His love for us. It also means we read His Word so we can acquire the real wisdom we need to be successful in the world. We also need to spend time meditating, reflecting on our actions, our experiences, and thinking through plans for our future. We plan and then we let God act and help us achieve those plans.

On your journey, don't forget to bring Jesus along as your companion. He will be there for you when you have to make the tough decisions, when you're tired and think you can't go on anymore. He will be your inner source of strength and encouragement. He will be there for you when no one else is. He will give you ideas, brilliant ideas on how to solve problems, how to create new things, how to mend a broken relationship, how to build teams, how to follow your leader, and how to lead your team. When you have a daily relationship with God, He will show you His vision for your life. He will show you the way and let you know when your mission is complete at every stage of the journey.

Final tips to be successful in the business world:

- Be prepared—physically, mentally, and spiritually—so when opportunities come you don't miss them.
- Continue to learn always—each job, every new responsibility you get, learn so you are ready for the next step.

- Have faith—believe in God and trust Him. Make the step. He will be there for you and with you along the way.
- Take others with you so you can enjoy the journey. Always include Jesus in your team!
- Plan ahead—you plan and God helps you get there. Without a plan you will get nowhere because you won't even know where you're going.
- Be a good follower and choose the mountain you want to climb. If you don't believe in the mission and vision of a company, don't join that company. Find one where your beliefs align with the organization. Otherwise, you'll have a hard time following.
- Climb your own mountain—you will always have choices. Ask God for the wisdom to discern which mountain to climb. Don't climb a mountain just because somebody else is doing it. Choose your own. Choose wisely and enjoy the journey!

ISAIAH 55: 8-9 (NLT): *"My thoughts are completely different from yours," says the Lord. "And my ways are far beyond anything you could imagine. For just as the heavens are higher than the earth, so are my ways higher than your ways and my thoughts higher than your thoughts."*

- **QUESTIONS TO PONDER**

  1. What does your mountain look like?
  2. How are you allowing God to help you climb your mountain?
  3. What are you doing to help others climb their mountains?

- **ACTION ITEMS**

  1. If you are already climbing your mountain, make sure you have all the tools (i.e., education, special skills, etc.)
  2. Allow God to help you along the way. You are not alone in your journey.
  3. Help one person climb their mountain and you will be blessed.

Part 2

—◂•▸—

YOUR CALLING

How to Connect the Two

Chapter 10

How I Found a Purpose in Every Job

When I was a little girl I used to love playing Monopoly with my siblings. I remember always wanting to be the bank. I liked distributing the initial money to all the players (my siblings) as I saw them as potential customers of *my* bank. I took my job seriously and arranged all the bills by denomination and all the bills facing the same way. I arranged all the cards for the homes by color, the houses by size, and stacked the insurance cards neatly in one corner of the Monopoly box.

I have never been a good loser. I always liked to win and had to learn the hard way (by my siblings asking me to leave the game if I didn't change my unacceptable behavior) how to deal with the situation when things (or the game in this instance) didn't go my way (meaning I didn't get to own the top producing properties such as the Railroad Stations). With time, and as I grew older, I learned self-control and to play as a good team player.

The first job I ever had was when I was sixteen years old at my mom's jewelry store in the Dominican Republic. I was her bookkeeper and started handling the inventory, sales, and cash drawer. I started enjoying working with the books of her business even though I had no formal training or really knew what I was doing. Even though I didn't know it at the time, God was preparing me for my first job once I came to the United States.

My second job was as a bilingual secretary for the principal of the university I was attending. Again, I didn't know it at the time, but God was preparing me for my second job in the United States.

In 1986 my family moved to Minnesota. I had completed eighteen months of college studies in Systems Engineering and Computer Science in the Dominican Republic. It was through the jewelry business my family was able to move to the United States legally. I had a working visa, which helped me find my first job. At first, I wasn't sure what kind of job I wanted or what I could be good at, but I knew three things I liked: people, computers, and money. After sharing what I liked with my new American friends, they encouraged me to look for a job as a bank teller. I didn't know what a "teller" did or "told" for that matter, but it sounded fun because it included the three things I enjoy.

I got my first job as a teller at Marquette Bank in downtown Minneapolis, after applying to many banks, having multiple interviews, and receiving several rejection letters. I used the little experience I had from working with my mom's business to feel comfortable in the interviews. I will never forget the last interview I had at Marquette Bank before they hired me. They asked if I was familiar with US currency.

I said yes.

Then they asked me if I had experience handling cash.

I said yes.

The next question was key. They asked me how much cash I was used to working with.

By now I was so experienced in interviewing for teller positions that I knew that the typical amount tellers were allowed to handle in their drawers was 10,000 dollars. So I said, "Well, I used to manage about 10,000 pesos."

I will have to admit that I exaggerated a little when I said 10,000 pesos. I usually only handled hundreds and sometimes a couple of thousand pesos. I have repented of this lie, and I don't recommend lying, so please don't follow my example.

I got the job. And for the first time, I realized there was a purpose in the job I had in my mom's business in Dominican Republic. She used to pay me with little gold rings that I was allowed to choose from her inventory. I still wear those little gold rings. They are precious to me, as they represent the first fruit of my labor and a gift from my mother.

There is a purpose in every job we hold—no matter how small or insignificant it may look or seem while we're doing it, or whether we realize it or recognize it at the time.

My goal with every job I've had is to love it. I've loved some jobs from the start. Others took a little time for me to really enjoy and learn to love. I loved my job as a teller. I loved the interaction with customers, treasured the friendships I developed with some of my customers (you know, the ones who will only go to *your* window and will even wait for you despite a long line). I enjoyed learning the computer system and handling money all day. Of course, there is no job without challenging days, and I had plenty of those, too.

I was a teller for eighteen months, and during that time I learned to handle the ordering of office supplies, balance the coin machine, handle mutilated money (the "mute" money that was sold to the Federal Reserve Bank when it was no longer usable), lead the teller sales team, and attend banking classes at night. My objective was to learn everything I could about the basics of banking and about my customers, and to prepare myself for my next job. My intention was never to stay as a teller. Don't get me wrong. Being a teller was fun, enjoyable, and rewarding. It is a very important job to have, as tellers are the face of the bank. But I'm the kind of person that, once I master a position, I have to move onto new things. Otherwise, I get bored. My goal was to be the best teller I could be. I am a competitive person but mostly with myself. I wanted to improve and learn more.

After one year, I started getting bored and decided I wanted to be a secretary. I chose that job as my next one because I thought if I could do secretarial duties in English that meant I really spoke the language. I started looking for a job at my bank as a secretary, and I met my future boss in the teller line. At the time, I didn't know who he was, and I merely treated him as I did all my customers.

Once again, my little job (which included answering phones in English and Spanish and typing correspondence in both languages) was enough experience to land my next job as secretary for five people in the cash management department. I absolutely loved my new job. My goal was to be the best secretary I could be and the best that department ever had.

You may ask, why have that goal? Why place such high expectations on yourself? Why not just be a secretary like all the others, do your job, and go home? Because I'm purposed to leave a legacy, a mark, wherever I go. Why do a mediocre job when I can do my best? I saw myself as an executive in training. I knew it would take years to achieve and earn the responsibilities that come with leadership positions in an organization. I knew I was young, inexperienced, and had a lot to learn—about banking and about business and about corporate America in general.

I notice that some (not all) young workers are not willing to wait and learn. They demand high-paying jobs and/or positions of leadership without acquiring the skills and experience necessary to handle those jobs. I, therefore, see the need to mentor the younger workers, and part of mentoring is teaching them to wait, be patient, and have appropriate expectations. When I was a young worker, I was just happy and grateful to God I had a job—in the United States!

While I was a secretary, I felt purposed to improve the job by making changes, to learn about the business of cash management, and to observe how the officers and sales people conducted themselves. I purposed to always do more than I was asked, to do tasks that those in higher positions did, without getting paid extra, and to learn other people's jobs.

Part of my job was to be the backup for my supervisor, the administrative assistant. This position was the liaison between the corporate customers and the bank's operations department. My goal was to do such a good job that if that person moved to a different job, I was the obvious choice for the promotion. And that is what happened. The person in that position moved to the operations department, and I was promoted after being a secretary for three years.

While I was the administrative assistant, I not only learned the job well, I became an expert, improved the job by automating processes, establishing procedures, and started doing tasks, such as sales proposals, that only the officers did previously. Even though I did not get paid to do the extra tasks, I decided it was great learning experience for me. Again, I loved this job and found my purpose for that position, which was preparing myself to be in sales while providing excellent customer service to my clients.

In early 1991, after one year in the administrative assistant position, I saw the need and an opportunity for a new position in the cash management department as customer service representative. I wrote the job description and gave the proposal to my boss with me as the only candidate. I may add that this happened while I was eight months pregnant with my second child; that was my biggest motivation for getting promoted. I told my boss, "You know, I'm going to have baby number two, which means I am going to need more money, which means I need to get promoted. I see this need in our department for a new position, and I think it would be a great opportunity for me. By the way, I'm your only candidate."

The position was approved and I got the promotion.

During 1992, after only a year of being the customer service representative, the announcement came out that my bank was sold to a large bank. The merger was to take place in January 1993. I found myself with two job offers: one with the purchasing bank as a customer service representative and one as a secretary to the president of a newly formed bank that the owners of the selling bank were planning to start. God had a purpose here that I didn't know about. He knew that the only way the purchasing bank would offer me a job was by me already being in the position of customer service. They needed someone to transition all the cash management customers to the new bank, and I was the only candidate. It was a very tough decision because I didn't want to leave my friends from the current bank. Marquette Bank was a mid-size community bank, and I was afraid of going to work for a very large national bank. I wasn't sure about what to do. What do I do when I have two good offers? I ask God for wisdom and, once He gives me the answer, I obey.

One night I was discussing my options with my husband, and he gave me the idea to counter offer the big bank—ask for twice the salary increase and twice the bonus amount they offered. My intention was not to be greedy but for the large bank to turn down my offer. I thought they would never accept because I was just the customer service rep, and who was I to counter offer the big bank anyway? I thought if they didn't accept the counter offer, it would make it easier for me to make my decision, and I would get to stay with the new startup bank, even though I didn't like the idea of going back to being a secretary. Well, I was wrong. The large bank accepted my offer and I had to go. I accepted the job and moved in faith, believing this move was God's will for me. I purposed to do the best I could to transition our corporate clients to the big bank.

Shortly after I started working at the new bank, I realized I did not fit in that environment. Did I make a mistake? Had I been led by greed? How could I make a difference in this big organization? What would my purpose be in this large company of thousands of employees? Was the Lord trying to teach me a lesson?

I don't believe I was led by greed because I actually didn't want them to accept my counter offer in the first place. While I met nice people at the large bank, I could not do only one thing—customer service. I wanted variety, and I couldn't do anything else other than my job nor could I help anybody else. The job was more of an assembly type environment, and I didn't fit.

After thinking and praying about it, I decided to call my previous boss to see if he could help me. He connected me up with his new boss, and I got a job offer as a private banking representative. Once again, I had to make a choice. This new job was a cut in pay, and no bonus was offered. If I had felt greed, it was gone by now, and I accepted the job. That was the only job I had that lasted only a short time. I felt bad leaving, but I was relieved and knew I made the right decision.

So what was God's plan all along? Why did He have me go through that painful experience? I believe it was His plan and will all along for me to go through the negotiation of the new job and to experience working in a large organization, because I learned many lessons. First, I will never again consider a job based on the money. There are other, more important things, to consider. For example, the environment, the people I work with, the customers I serve, the learning opportunities I may have, and the future career opportunities.

I learned a lot during the five months and eight days (not that I was counting) I spent at that large bank. I learned about cash management processes in a big bank. I learned about what happens to customers and employees through an acquisition—the challenges for both sides. I learned to appreciate our customers—the main reason we are in business to begin with.

I learned about myself as well—the type and size of organization I like to work in, the need to have variety in my job, the tasks I like and don't like doing, and the type of environment and management style I flourish under, among other things. In addition to all of the things I learned, I got to keep the bonus I received, so I believe it was definitely in God's plan for me to take that step. He had a purpose, which I discovered.

My adventures in banking and learning opportunities continued with my newly created position as private banking representative. I was learning about the consumer side of banking. My objective in this job was to be the best rep I could be. Therefore, I read all the brochures, memorized all the types of accounts we offered, learned the computer system, and started working with lending officers. I started familiarizing myself with the lending terms and products.

In 1995 the bank decided to introduce a new product in the market: online banking. It was new territory for our bank since we were the first community bank to offer this technology. I saw a tremendous opportunity to work with technology and provide a great new product to our customers.

I proposed to senior management the idea of a brand new job—online banking specialist. I wrote the job description and proposed myself as the perfect candidate. The position was approved!

I was promoted to online banking specialist and kept my duties as private banking rep. The promotion came with a raise, too. My job was to help customers get a better handle on their finances by bringing their bank information directly to their computers, giving them the convenience of paying their bills electronically. I became an expert on this product. My sales ratio after giving a demonstration was 95 percent. My first goal was to sign up all the executives and owners of the bank. I knew if they used the product, they would embrace it, promote it, and help me succeed. It worked! I not only signed them up and trained them on how to use the system, but I developed a personal relationship with the top leaders in my organization and they got to know me as a person, not just as an employee.

This job was one of the best and most enjoyable jobs in banking I've ever had. Even though my goal was simple—to help my customers with their banking, God had bigger reasons for having me in that position. He rewarded me with many friendships, new knowledge of banking technology, and extra visibility in the organization, which I was not expecting. I had the privilege of working with the entire group of lending officers and all their private banking customers.

During this time, I decided I wanted to work more in sales instead of in a supporting role. I wanted to have my own portfolio of customers I could service and take care of. To be considered for a position of private banking officer, I started taking self-study courses in consumer lending, studied the bank's credit and loan policies, and made cold calls to potential private banking customers such as attorneys, accountants, and other professionals. The hardest part of cold calling wasn't making the call; it was giving away the new customers to a lender. Because I was not a lender yet, I could not have a portfolio of customers. After several months of cold calling prospects, it finally happened. I was promoted to private banking officer. As our bank grew, the more experienced lenders gave me some of their customers so I was able to start my portfolio.

I continued my duties as an online banking specialist and worked with all the lenders' customers. I loved this job!

I felt useful and needed by my bank colleagues and by my customers.

With my newly formed portfolio of customers, my goal now was to service them, anticipate their needs, deepen my relationships with them, and sell the bank's products.

I will describe my home life at this point to help you understand the next transition at work. As mentioned before, when I moved to the United States in 1986, I had only completed eighteen months of a degree in Systems Engineering and Computer Science in the Dominican Republic. I met my husband on New Year's Eve of 1986, and we were married in July 1988. We had our first child in 1989, and our second child in the spring of 1991. During those years, I worked full-time and my husband also worked full-time while attending college full-time. He graduated in December 1991, and we decided it was time for me to go back to college to finish my degree. I finished my Associates in Arts degree from North Hennepin Community College in 1996.

In early 1997 I wanted to finish my undergraduate degree in business or finance, but it was not God's will. My husband wanted me to spend more time with our kids, so I reluctantly agreed to wait. I knew in my heart he was right, and it wasn't the right time for me to go back.

After obeying God by choosing not to go back to school, I said to Him in my prayer, "Okay, Lord, you'll just have to promote me without a degree."

Two months later, my manager came to my office and said, "Marci, let's talk management." The Lord immediately reminded me of my prayer, and I accepted the position of branch manager for Marquette Capital Bank, downtown Minneapolis.

I knew this position would be challenging because the bank fired the previous manager three months prior to my start. There was nobody to train me. I moved to an empty desk with no one to tell me what to do. Employee morale was very low, and there was a lot of confusion. My new goal became to learn how to manage a retail branch and restore the morale of my new employees. This was one of the most challenging jobs I ever had, and the most difficult up until that point in my career.

In my heart, from 1986 when I came to the United States until 1998, my career was my priority. I was determined to succeed. There is nothing wrong with wanting to succeed and, as an immigrant, I especially value and appreciate that desire. However, there is something wrong with having your first or top priority be any career.

I had arrived at a fork in the road—a crucial time in my life, a turning point in my career and in my spiritual life, my walk with the Lord. I had to make a decision. What was my top priority in my life: God or my career? I chose God and changed my priorities forever to be: God, my family, then my work or career. At that point, I left my career, as it were, and started seeking God to help me put Him first in my life.

My first step was to talk to my manager, so I set up a meeting in the early summer of 1998. I told her I wanted to spend more time with my family and to work fewer hours. I told her I knew this meant I had to step down from the branch manager position. I also told her I could always go back to manage a branch, but I could never regain these years with my children. I also suggested an idea for a new part-time job as online banking specialist for the region. I wanted to work fewer hours and be able to pick up my kids after school. I was willing to work from home, if necessary, to get my new job done.

Once again I wrote a new job description, we proposed the job, and it was approved. The plan was to start working 8:00 a.m. to 2:30 p.m., so I could pick up my kids from school and spend the afternoon with them. I started my new schedule when school started that year and continued managing the branch while we were looking for my replacement. The new position was approved, and I was to start in early 1999 with the new budget year.

Even though I was excited about this new position, I had no peace in my heart because I saw the potential of being at a client's site when it was time to pick up my kids at school. What would I do? So I talked with my husband, and I decided it was time to change careers and leave banking altogether. I decided to move to the information technology (IT) field, which I also liked.

For a couple of years, my husband and I had been volunteering at our kids' school in an IT parent focus group. Our church owned the school. My job as a volunteer was to train the school teachers on how to use their computers. At one of the meetings, I felt the Lord urging me to tell the focus group leader that I was interested in the position of Y2K project manager the church was going to have available the following year. I finally had the courage to tell the leader about my interest in the position, and she got very excited. I told her I couldn't leave the bank until after December 31 so I could earn my bonus and that I had to wait until the first week in March so I would get it paid. She said, "Perfect, because I can't hire you anyway until that very week when the new church's budget starts."

On March 5, 1999, I received my bonus, and I received a job offer from the church as Y2K project manager. I was very sad to leave the bank because I loved my coworkers and my customers. But I felt strongly in my heart I had to make this change for the sake of my family and also to make God my first priority.

I left the bank in March of 1999 and started working for the church, which was a 501(c)3 nonprofit charitable organization. Once again, I found myself in a new position with no one to teach me or tell me what to do. I had to make it up myself. The only preparation I had was my attendance in college more than ten years before, some classes I took on programming at IBM school, and a computer and networking course I decided to study the last three months I was at the bank, called A+ certification. However, I did have my husband who is an IT professional and who had already been advising the church's focus group leader (now my boss) for several years.

My first three months in this job gave me the opportunity to meet the entire staff of 330 employees of our church. I conducted interviews in the various areas to learn about the church's systems and processes so I could prepare a plan for the year 2000. My goal in this position was to learn everything I could as fast as I could about the ministry, about IT, and come up with a plan to successfully transition the church into the new millennium.

After six months in this position, the head of finance passed away and the senior pastor of the church asked my boss to move into that position. He then asked me to step up as the director of IT in October of 1999. 1 had negotiated a part-time position working thirty-seven hours per week instead of the fifty-plus that I was working at the bank.

While I was concerned that my hours would increase, I managed somehow to keep the hours under control. My husband became my main IT advisor.

My plan as the head of the IT department was to continue to learn about technologies, networking, and computer systems in addition to learning how things worked in the ministry and the nonprofit world.

In June of 2001, after only eighteen months, my manager, the associate of finance, decided to retire. A few weeks earlier, I was walking in the hallway, and I heard a voice clearly telling me, "You will be an associate." I know this sounds crazy, but I heard it and I knew it was God. I immediately rebuked those words because I knew it would be more work, and I didn't want to have the additional responsibilities. There were five associates who were the top leaders of the church under the senior pastor. Nevertheless, I told God I was willing to do whatever He needed me to do.

Because of my previous banking experience, the senior pastor offered me the job of associate of finance in charge of finance, human resources, and information technology. After praying about it, I felt God wanted me to take the position even though it was going to be full-time again. Although I was concerned about the amount of responsibility this position carried, I had peace that God was going to help me and equip me to do it. My new goal became to establish policies and procedures for these areas, to centralize, standardize, and formalize these departments at the church. I also desired to do the best I could to continue to learn about the ministry life and how nonprofits worked.

During the next three-and-one-half years (2001 to 2004) I learned more than how to operate a nonprofit charitable organization; I learned how to hear the voice of God and how to trust Him every step of the way. I implemented many changes, automated many processes, and turned those departments around so they could better serve the rest of the church. My departments were the backbone, the infrastructure of the ministry, and they had to be well run. As a thirty million gross revenue church, it had to be run like a large corporation. I learned about human resources and continued to learn about IT.

Early in 2004, a desire to go back to banking grew in me. Once again I was faced with a tough decision. I loved the people I worked with at the church, but I felt in my heart that God had other plans for me. After almost one year of praying and seeking God about this decision, I decided to go back to banking.

In the summer of 2004, my previous boss from cash management told me he left his previous employment as president of a bank to start a new bank and he asked me to join him in his new venture. This had been his dream. I cheered for him and told him, "Finally you will be able to start your own bank and fulfill your dream."

He thanked me because I had been, up to that point, the only friend who had encouraged him to do that and to follow his heart. One Sunday afternoon, a couple of months later, the Lord encouraged me to call my former boss, and I did. I told him I had a desire to go back to banking but this time I wanted to be the CFO of the bank and learn to run a bank as a business instead of working as a lender.

After several conversations, he offered me the job of chief financial officer in charge of the finance, operations, IT, and human resources departments. In addition, I became the corporate secretary of the board of directors of the bank and the holding company.

I was sad to announce my decision to the senior pastor, whom I respect and love. I said, "Just as some people are called to faraway countries as missionaries, I am called to corporate America as my mission field." With that, he gave me his blessing, and we parted ways in good terms.

I left the church at the end of 2004 and started working on the bank startup in January 2005. The president and directors raised the capital, and the bank opened in July 2005. My initial goal was to help my boss, the president of the bank, fulfill his dream of starting a bank from scratch, to see it grow successfully, and to know that I'm running the bank while he's selling the bank's products to our customers. My goal, as the bank grew, was to create shareholder value by protecting the bank's capital and its assets while creating an environment where the employees can flourish and be successful. I was a shareholder of this bank and, as with all my previous jobs, I wanted to leave a legacy and a mark in this organization and in the lives of the people I touched.

You see, I was now an executive with a lot of responsibilities. I found a reason for me to be in every job I've ever had, and that gave me the drive to learn and succeed, which gave me a purpose. During the first nine years since starting the bank, I was promoted from vice president to senior vice president to executive vice president. In addition, I was promoted to chief operating officer, and served as chief financial officer. I went back to school in 2009 and finished my undergraduate degree in Business Management in 2011. I call it "my 27-year degree" because that's how long it took me to finish!

In January 2014, my role as EVP/COO/CFO was split into two jobs due to the bank's growth. I was able to promote all my employees to the next level and promoted one of them to the CFO position. My new job became EVP/COO and now CRO (chief risk officer). God had a purpose for me in every job, and I believe He has a purpose for every job you ever have as well. God prepared me through the years to take me where I am today.

Again, after almost one year of praying and seeking God to show me my next step, I decided to leave the bank. I announced it to the current bank president almost to the day ten years after I told the founding president, "Let's do it. Let's start the bank."

I left the bank on September 30, 2014, and decided to start a bank consulting practice helping community banks be successful by establishing a strong foundation and infrastructure across the board. I began working with community banks that need strategic planning, enterprise risk management, and talent management expertise. I wanted to duplicate what I created and developed throughout the ten years I was at the startup bank and help other community banks in the years to come. That will be part of my legacy I leave when I retire from my banking career.

In my good-bye speech to the bank staff before I left, I told them, "If people ask you what Marci is going to do next, tell them that she's going to pursue her dreams—all of them."

In addition of starting my bank consulting practice, I'm pursuing a public speaking career, writing more books, and volunteering on nonprofit boards. I want to inspire others to find their gifts and pursue their calling by connecting their gifts to what they do in their careers. I want to encourage others not to wait anymore. Now is the time. Every day, as people prepare, they can pursue and do their calling.

I don't know for sure what's in store for me in the future, but I do know that God continues to prepare me for what's to come.

PSALM 37:23-24 (NLT) *The Lord directs the steps of the godly. He delights in every detail of their lives. Though they stumble, they will never fall, for the Lord holds them by the hand.*

- QUESTIONS TO PONDER

  1. What are some purposes you have found in your jobs during your working life?
  2. What was your reason for going to school to study your degree?
  3. What things interest you about the field you're in right now?

- ACTION ITEMS

  1. Write down what things you have enjoyed most in your past jobs and in your current job.
  2. List what you have learned in past jobs that helps you in your current job.
  3. Share your goals with someone you trust. Your goals will come alive in you again, which will give you renewed purpose in your job.

Chapter 11

How I Found My Purpose in Life

During my last year working at the church, I started asking God to show me His purpose for my life. I wanted to know what my personal purpose in life was, my calling. Why did He create *me*? How could I fulfill all that He has for me in my life? What is His plan and will for my life? After much searching in my heart, praying, and continually asking God to show me, I was finally able to put into writing what I believe my mission and purpose in life is. My mission is to *help working people be successful*. I help people by providing inspiration, encouragement, and leadership.

In that process, I found out what my mission field is. Some people are called to distant lands such as India, China, or Africa. My personal mission field is right here in America—the business world (for profit and nonprofit). That's where God needs me, where my gifts can develop, and I can continue to serve God.

During all these years I have been working, I always find myself helping other people (men, women, younger and older, superiors and subordinates) by encouraging them to be the best they can be. I always want to help people be successful and, at the same time, obtain the balance they want in their lives. People come to me when they lose their jobs, asking for help with their resumes, help connecting them with other people who could potentially employ them, and sometimes asking me to pray for them during the transition. My friends call and ask me to help them with ideas on what types of jobs they may be good at, because they trust my opinion.

I ask them several questions that help them reveal their gifts, what skills they have, what they're good at, and what they don't like or don't enjoy about it. I ask them hard questions and give them homework to follow up on so they can search in their hearts for what it is they want to do with their lives and careers. I was doing all of this from my heart because I have a burning desire to help others with their careers and see them succeed. God showed me how He is using my gifts already and how the passion I have was given to me by Him. I use the gift God gave me to encourage others daily.

Leadership is another gift that God gave me, and I use it wherever I have an opportunity. Whether that is in a leadership position at work, or as a volunteer, or just helping my friends find their way in the sea of career choices, I help by leading them in the right direction.

When I share my personal story and people hear how God has helped me find my purpose in every job and every part of my life, they are inspired. People want to hear inspiring stories. However, there is a fine line between getting excited by sharing a story with the purpose of showing how good God is and thinking I'm the big deal and it's all my own doing. That is a matter of the heart. I believe that if my heart is right with God, the story will convey the right motive.

People will be inspired and will not feel inferior or think I am bragging.

I hope that by sharing my stories, you will be inspired to share your own story with others. I hope you seek God to help you find your own purpose in life. When you ask God to reveal your purpose in life and your calling, take time and use patience searching in your own heart. Spend the time you need seeking God and looking into your heart, and it will come. You will find your purpose in life. You will find your calling.

PHILIPPIANS **3:14 (KJV)** *I press toward the mark for the prize of the high calling of God in Christ Jesus.*

- QUESTIONS TO PONDER

  1. What is your purpose in life?
  2. Have you talked to God about it?
  3. How often do you share your story with others?

- ACTION ITEMS

  1. Write down what you believe is your purpose in life.
  2. Seek God with all your heart and ask Him to reveal His purpose for your life.
  3. Once you find your purpose, share it with others.

Chapter 12

The Corporate World—
A Ripe Mission Field

As I explained in the previous chapter, my mission is in the corporate world. That's where I feel God called me to harvest souls and help working people be successful. That's where I can fulfill my calling.

I took awhile to consider the business world as a mission field. This was a revelation to my heart. I have never gone on a mission trip before, but you don't need to go overseas to participate in a mission trip. Just look around and you will see the biggest field is within your reach. You just have to prepare your heart to help people come to Christ. You have to be humble, knowledgeable about the Word of God, and knowledgeable about business so you can connect with the businesspeople God puts on your path. The hearts of the people in the corporate world, just as any other mission field, are ready to be harvested, but God needs laborers in those places. Are you one of those laborers?

Sometimes I feel guilty that I am not called (or don't feel called) to go to other countries to preach the Gospel of Jesus Christ. But God has shown me that He needs people everywhere to be a light to others. My purpose is to influence people right where I am, in the marketplace. That's where God needs me.

I want to inspire and encourage you to be content if you are called to the business world because that is where God needs you. Whether you are called to be a leader or a worker within an organization, it doesn't matter. God still needs you. If you are to become a leader in an organization, the road to the top is not easy, but you can do it with God's help. Corporate America needs godly leaders but it also needs godly workers. In this chapter, I offer tips to succeed in the corporate world—both as a worker starting out and as an executive, if that's how far God wants you to go.

Publications of every kind talk about widespread white collar crime that has overwhelmed our country. What has gone wrong? Where did we take a wrong turn? What has happened to the corporate leaders of America? What are their moral standards and how are those standards affecting the entire country? Who are we to follow if we want to go into the corporate world? How do we identify the true, solid character leaders we want to imitate? Unfortunately, white collar crime is not new. You may agree that our corporate standards are not the ones we are proud of as a country.

How does an organization change for the better? How do we implement new ideas, new ways of doing things? It comes from the top. But if the top leaders are corrupt, then the corrupt ways are disseminated like a dirty river that flows from the top of the mountains all the way down into the valleys. But godly leaders can change an organization.

If you are at the bottom of the corporate mountain and feel called to be in leadership, the hike up can be very difficult—like being in a river swimming upstream. It can be exhausting and even deadly. So how do you get to the top of an organization? How do you become part of the decision-making executive team?

Some ways are by working hard, making connections along the way that will give you a lift, by helping others, and by listening and following God's advice.

Are there shortcuts to the top in an established organization?

There is only one, in my opinion, that comes from God and that is favor—favor with both men and God. When you put your trust in God, He will make a way for you. He connects you with the right people at the right time. He promotes you His way. Is it automatic? No, it takes years of preparation, education, acquiring skills, and building your network. It takes time to build your reputation as an executive.

Not everyone is meant to be a corporate leader, and not everyone is meant to be an executive. Being a leader and an executive is hard work and an immense responsibility. Knowing how to lead people is a gift from God. Leaders have the obligation to cultivate, recognize, and develop their skills.

Corporate America can change if we have leaders who are men and women of integrity, people of their word, and people of character with no personal agenda except to serve others. Leaders need humility and the knowledge that God put them in those places of authority.

If you believe God has called you to the corporate world as your mission field, regardless of your occupation or position in the organization, start preparing to work as God's laborer. Nurture humility, because to influence people at the top you have to work very closely with others. God may promote you to places you never dreamed of being part of. He may put you in circles of people you don't know, and He may ask you to take certain positions at work you are not very comfortable with, yet. You may feel inadequate or out of place, but that's okay. God has equipped you with some gifts that you haven't used or developed until now.

How do you nurture humility so God can work through you? I believe the best way is to always have a thankful heart, a heart of gratitude toward God. Always recognize it is Him who gives you the promotions, the opportunities, and the connections. When you experience success, get on your knees and thank God—that's how your heart will stay humble.

God has opened doors for me to be promoted many times throughout my career. I am thankful for each promotion and have recognized the hand of God in each situation. I spend time on Saturday mornings praying and asking God to keep me humble, because I know I am nothing without Him.

The next tool you need as a laborer in the corporate world is to know the Word of God well enough to help others. How do you prepare and increase in the knowledge of God's Word? The best way is by reading the Bible daily, even if it's just one verse or two a day. Having the Word of God in your mind and close to your heart will help you at the moments when you need to share His Word with others. He will remind you of a certain scripture at the appropriate time, and His peace will reign in your heart. Choose some scriptures from the Bible and memorize them, or bookmark them in your smartphone, or write them down. Repeat them in your head when you are in a difficult situation at work or when you are feeling inadequate. For example, remember Romans 12:4-5 (NLT), which says, "Just as our bodies have many parts and each part has a special function, so it is with

Christ's body. We are many parts of one body, and we all belong to each other." This scripture helped me understand a situation when I was an IT director and I needed my team's expertise on a server issue. God reminded me that I could lead the team, while they could use their technical knowledge to get the job done.

If God promotes you to a position of leadership, take the responsibility seriously, but also remember He put you there, and He will help you be successful. Remember what God told Joshua when he had to lead the people of Israel into the Promised Land in Joshua 1:5 (NLT), "… For I will be with you as I was with Moses. I will not fail you or abandon you."

When I was promoted to branch manager, I had to rely on this promise because there was no one to train me. God did not leave me. He put people in my path to help me learn my new role at the bank. My part was to be humble enough to start calling those people and ask for help.

Another important element of work in the corporate world as God's laborer is to have business knowledge. There are several ways you can become knowledgeable about business. One way is to obtain education. Finish high school and then go on to college. Pursue your education before you get married and start having a family, because it only becomes more difficult later—though it can be done. This applies to both men and women. Most people in business are educated and expect to relate to others who are also educated. Because of my personal situation, I had to interrupt my college several times, and it was very difficult to finally finish my undergraduate degree. It was hard, but not impossible. Many people nowadays do it while working and raising a family.

Whether or not you have a college degree, continue to educate yourself and learn by attending seminars, reading business publications and books about various industries. Another way is to make friends and establish connections in various industries, especially the one you're most interested in pursuing.

Once you obtain a job in the industry you want to be part of, build your skills through each job you have—from the very first one and going forward as you grow in your career. Sometimes you need to make lateral moves and even step back to gain valuable experience to progress in your career and obtain your goals. As you are promoted to higher levels of responsibility, God will give you opportunities to influence your superiors, peers, and your subordinates.

Influencing people is not as easy as it sounds. Because our culture and workplace are sensitive to language and behavior that can be perceived as offensive, you will need to be careful about how you try to influence others. The best practice is to be a positive role model with your conduct—how you react to situations, how you treat people, and how you behave both in public as well as in private. Being a person of integrity and living a life of truth and honesty is the example God needs you to be in this mission field. At the same time, being a person of strong character, someone who is not moved or easily persuaded to do the wrong thing, is crucial to being successful in this mission field. Having high moral standards is critical. Avoid being influenced by other's opinions of what you should do or not do. Always follow your own heart, and do what's ethical and moral, not what's convenient or what "everyone else" is doing.

Just as farmers need tools to harvest their crops, you too need the tools God provides. First, find out what those tools are, then learn how to use them, and finally utilize them for their intended purpose. These tools are the armor of God, as the apostle Paul describes in detail in his letter to the Ephesians.

As you can see, God gives us responsibilities and tasks, but He also gives us tools and armor to protect us and prepare us to fulfill our calling.

EPHESIANS 6:13–18 (NLT), *Use every piece of God's armor to resist the enemy in the time of evil, so that after the battle you will still be standing firm. Stand your ground, putting on the sturdy belt of truth and the body armor of God's righteousness. For shoes, put on the peace that comes from the Good News, so that you will be fully prepared. In every battle you will need faith as your shield to stop the fiery arrows aimed at you by Satan. Put on salvation as your helmet, and take the sword of the Spirit, which is the word of God. Pray at all times and on every occasion in the power of the Holy Spirit. Stay alert and be persistent in your prayers for all Christians everywhere.*

- **QUESTIONS TO PONDER**

  1. In what ways do you feel God may be calling you to be a laborer in your mission field?
  2. What are you doing to prepare to be a successful laborer?
  3. If you believe you are called to the business world but know you are not called to lead a corporation, what are you doing as a laborer of God in your current position?

- **ACTION ITEMS**

  1. Write down a list of situations where God used you to help others in your work. Doing this will give you momentum to continue to do His work in the business world whether you are at the top or not.
  2. List the people you can influence within your company both up (your boss, your company leaders), down (your employees if you are in management or other employees in entry level positions), or at your same level (your peers), and outside your company (vendors, customers, clients, shareholders). Start working on your list and exercise your influence.
  3. Thank God for the position you hold in the business world, because you are important to Him and to fulfilling His plan on earth.

Chapter 13

Achieving Your Purpose and High Calling

W e all have dreams and desires that may seem impossible to attain. We need to remember that these are dreams and desires that God Himself put in our hearts. I believe that what He starts by giving us those desires, He will finish by helping us attain them.

The first thing to do is to seek God and ask Him to reveal to your heart the purpose for your life and the high calling. He will give you the revelation through His Holy Spirit. Search into your heart, and you will find desires, like little treasures, ready to be discovered that He placed in you. These treasures need first to be discovered, then you need to take hold of them, appropriate them, and take ownership of them. Take them out from the hidden places of your heart and into the light. Some of these treasures are dusty and some, like old treasures, have gotten dirty with time. You need to clean them first. God helps you do that with His love, mercy, and tenderness. Take care of your gifts and guard them.

There are some hidden treasures that only God can bring out of you at the appropriate time. Those are unique desires He has placed in you. Once these desires are brought into the light, ask God what do to with each one and how to use them for His Kingdom. The next step is to wait on Him with patience. Sometimes He will tell you right away because your heart is ready to receive. Other times He will wait to reveal to you the bigger plan when you are ready.

In the meantime, while you wait, continue to prepare yourself both naturally (physically, emotionally, and mentally) and spiritually. Always continue to learn in both realms. Your brain needs development, training, and exercise. It is the same with your spirit.

Before you can step up to the high calling of God in your life, your heart needs to be ready. Your motives need to be pure, and you have only one goal: to serve God and give Him all the glory. Paul says in Philippians 4:13 (NLT), "For I can do everything with the help of Christ who gives me the strength I need."

Your entire life is preparation for your high calling. You can also walk in your high calling as you prepare. Walk in faith one step at a time. When you are living in His will for your life, your whole life is preparation for the next step, and everything you do is part of a bigger plan. Don't underestimate little things—tasks and steps needed to go through in order to achieve a higher purpose. He gives you signs and hints along the way that you can learn to recognize and obey when He gives you the signal to do so. Philippians 3:14 (KJV) says, "I press toward the mark for the prize of the high calling of God in Christ Jesus." Only in His presence will you be able to recognize the marks, the signals, the next steps. Psalm 37:23 (KJV) says, "The steps of a righteous man are ordered by the Lord, and He delighteth in his way."

Once you have the steps, He will give you the next marks (or signals) and direct your path. You can achieve your dreams only with Him because He is a part of each dream, and He put them in your heart to begin with.

As I have been writing this book, God has been helping me step into my life's calling. My mission, to "help working people be successful," sounds simple, but it took me years to put into one sentence what I felt in my heart that I was called to do. What I mean by "working people," I mean all the people in the corporate or business world (my mission field and my niche). When I mean "successful" I mean in every way and in every aspect of their lives.

Sometimes I help people by reviewing their resumes, connecting them with others for a new job, coaching them to get ready for an interview, or brainstorming with them about a career change. Other times I help working people by praying with them, and for them when I'm at a distance. I help others identify their callings by first discovering their gifts. There are some tools, like the Strengths Finder™ that help people identify their unique strengths. The unique talents that God gives each person, along with their unique life experiences, help define their callings and how they can serve the Kingdom of God. I help usher people go through that process.

With my new company, Malzahn Strategic, I help banks be more successful by implementing a strong organizational infrastructure and operational efficiencies. I use my years of experience in banking to help community banks be successful and remain alive while competing with larger institutions. I connect them with nonprofit organizations. My other passion in life is to help nonprofits be successful by helping them achieve their individual missions. Do you see how God is utilizing all my strengths, gifts, and experiences to help me fulfill my calling in life? He has prepared me all my life, and I look forward to continuing my journey with Him while I fulfill my calling.

PSALM 37:4 (NLT) *Take delight in the Lord, and He will give you your heart's desires.*

- **QUESTIONS TO PONDER**

  1. What is your high calling? If you don't know yet, it's time to find out.
  2. In what ways is your current job preparing you for your high calling?
  3. In what ways does a job you want instead relate to your high calling in life?

- **ACTION ITEMS**

  1. Ask God to place desires in your heart that He wants for you. Ask Him to take away worldly desires and replace them with godly desires.
  2. When you discover those desires, make sure your motives are pure.
  3. Ask God to make those desires a reality and to help you achieve your dreams.

Chapter 14

With a Purpose, There Is No Glass Ceiling

When you discover your purpose or calling, God will open doors that no man or woman can shut. When you have a purpose, you see beyond the obstacles in front of you and you will go through, around, or over them. You work through the issues and have the courage to move on despite circumstances.

For so many years, I didn't understand what the glass ceiling really was until I had a picture of it in my mind. The glass ceiling is like a physical ceiling above your head that you cannot crack or go through. It is strong and thick, but you can see clearly what is on the other side. You can see other people above you. You can see the positions they hold, and you can see them walking over you. You can see them planning and making decisions for your company that will eventually affect you personally. You can speak as loud as you want, but they don't hear you.

I had some questions: Can those people see you from above when they look down? Can they see you waving, making noise, and running around beneath them? Do those people observe the employees under the see-through floor?

Or do they hold themselves up as superior and want that floor to stay sealed? Are there hidden ways, secret doors, unopened cracks where some people could get through? If you could indeed get through and get up to that level, would you be able to do it unharmed? Or would there be scars and compromises you would have to make in order to make it up there?

Frustration comes when you feel you can't do anything about the glass ceiling except watch and be the victim of the decisions made by those above that glass ceiling. However, there is much you can do from below to make a difference. First, there are some questions you need to ask God about and also ask of yourself. Where does He want you to be at this time in your life? Where do you find yourself right now? I believe the corporate business world is made out of several layers with each having its own glass ceiling. Looking up from the bottom level, you can probably see the many ceilings above you, and it all becomes confusing, like a maze.

Most people start at some lower level in an organization. You can't realistically expect to be placed at the top when you are young and inexperienced. Getting to the top takes effort, knowledge, experience, contacts, skills, and many other attributes. There are other questions you need answered as well: Do you *want* to be at the top? Are you *called* to be at the top, in a senior position, leading an organization? Do you have what it takes to lead? Leadership is a gift given to people by God and with that gift comes a lot of responsibility. Romans 12:8 (NLT) says, "... If God has given you leadership ability, take the responsibility seriously." Do you believe you are one of them and are you ready to step up and follow your calling in leadership?

We can all be leaders in some circumstances and lead some people during the course of our lives, but being called to lead a company is a unique gift. Some entrepreneurs may be excellent at what they do in their vocation but may not be good leaders, so they fail when they try to run companies.

Understanding in your heart about your own leadership abilities and desires from the beginning will help you avoid frustration as you grow in your career. Some people are called to work under the leadership of others. There is nothing wrong with that. You just need to know where your place is at any given time in your life. Good leaders are also good followers. Every leader, at some point in his or her life, was a follower. Even when you get to the top, you still have to answer to God and need to be a follower of Jesus. Always remember that as you move up in your career.

There are plenty of things you can do while you wait to crack that glass ceiling. First of all, you need to have a good attitude toward your work, your company, and your leaders. If you are serious about getting to the top, then you need to start acquiring the skills necessary to lead an organization, learn the industry, research, study, obtain the needed certifications, or whatever is necessary to become a leader there. Next, you need to create and build a network of people who will help you get there. These people can be your coworkers, boss, mentor, sponsor, and other counselors and friends who can help you achieve your goals. Spiritually speaking, you need to grow in the Lord so you can obtain and grow your leadership skills God's way. He can direct your path, train you personally on the things you need to change, and touch your heart to be compassionate toward others in a way that only He can do.

You also need to understand the reason you want to be at the top of your organization, either in the company where you currently work or in your own business. Why do you want to be the top leader? Why do you want to lead an organization? What is your purpose in doing so? Wanting to make a difference is not enough. Each of us can make a difference at any level in an organization and in our communities. Also important is to have a vision of where you're going and where you want to take the people who report to you, the ones who work under your direction. A caring heart for all employees and stakeholders is a requirement.

Being at the top is not about you. It's about other people. It's about making a difference from a position of authority and influencing others positively by being a person of integrity and character. It's about taking responsibility not only for your own actions and decisions but for the people you lead as well.

Glass ceilings do exist and are real. However, when you are in the will of God for your life and this is your gift and desire, He prepares you—both professional as well as spiritually—to occupy one of those top leadership positions. History shows that women have had to fight to crack the glass ceiling and so have people of color. But the ceiling is cracked now and the opening is widening, creating opportunities for many more people than before.

The questions are: What are you going to do when you go through the glass ceiling? Will you turn your back on those behind you? Or will you look through the floor beneath you and help others come up? Will you observe future leaders develop and help them by connecting them with the right people and mentoring them? Or will you say, "Tough. They have to fight just as I did in order to get up here"?

Below are some tips on how to crack the glass ceiling:

If you prefer to not go through the ranks and through many glass ceilings in a business organization, you may want to start your own company. You'll be the top leader. But make sure you don't create a glass ceiling for others in your company.

If you are starting out your career or are at the bottom of the organization and want to achieve more, don't despair. With time you will grow and, as you learn, you will acquire more experience. Start making connections and networking with people who can connect you with leaders in your company. This is easier to do in a smaller company than in a large corporation, but it can be done in either.

Plan the career path you want to take. Once you have done that, start getting to know people in the organization and in the industry who can help you succeed. Seek mentors who can give you advice along the way and help you improve in your role. Choose mentors carefully as they can have great influence in your life. They can connect you with other decision-makers and recommend you for promotions. Mentors can become your sponsors, which is a step beyond a mentor. Choose a person you respect and admire, someone more experienced than you in your chosen area or industry.

Accept roles of responsibility that will give you visibility in your work and in your community. Usually, assisting or leading a fundraising event for a nonprofit organization (perhaps one that your company supports) is a great way to gain visibility. Volunteering for projects that are beyond your set of responsibilities will give you opportunities to be noticed by other leaders in your company, not just your boss.

Compete only with yourself. Don't step over other people or backstab your friends and coworkers in order to get a promotion or the next job you want. If the promotion is in God's will for your life, it will happen. If you insist on doing it your way, it will probably not work out. Compete only with yourself when you continue to learn and do things to improve yourself. Join organizations where you can volunteer and acquire skills you don't have the opportunity to develop where you currently work, or go back to school and obtain further education.

Most importantly, ask God to help you crack any glass ceiling above you. Ask Him for the right tools and how to use them at the right time. If you really feel in your heart that you want to be in top leadership, ask Him to give you the desire of your heart and He will. Ask Him to show you ways you can improve yourself and ways you can change and grow as a person. Ask Him to put you in positions where He can get the glory—not you, places where you can be of greater service to Him—not with the intention of attaining personal benefit from power and influence. Seek God with all your heart so you can know with certainty His will for your life. Trust God to know that where you are now is exactly where He wants you to be, and ask Him to give you patience while you wait.

When you involve God in your work life, He opens doors to opportunities that no one can shut. He gives you favor with key people in your company, people who have the power and influence to promote you and bring you along. Give God a chance to direct your path, and you will see how He not only gives you the tools to go through the glass ceiling, but also how He can make the glass ceiling disappear altogether, like fog goes away when the sun comes up in the morning. If you are called to be at the top, God will make a way. Like the sunlight, He will show you the way, the path to follow. Like the heat that comes with the sun, He will melt away the roadblocks that are in your way.

DEUTERONOMY 1:13 (NLT) *Choose some men from each tribe who have wisdom, understanding, and a good reputation, and I will appoint them as your leaders.*

- **QUESTIONS TO PONDER**

  1. In what ways have you experienced the glass ceiling in your life?
  2. How can you help others as you go up the corporate ladder and once you arrive at your destination?
  3. How are you using the relationships you currently have to help you crack the glass ceiling?

- **ACTION ITEMS**

  1. If you don't know for sure the role you want in your company, ask God today to reveal His purpose for you in your work.
  2. If God's will for you is to go to the top, then start working on the tips mentioned above so you can serve Him in that capacity when the time comes.
  3. If God's will for you is to stay where you are and not be a senior leader of a company, be content and be the best employee that company can have. Work as unto God in whatever position He needs you to be in.

Chapter 15

What to Do When You Lose Your Purpose at Work

When starting a new job or career, we feel charged up and energized. We come to the new situation with new ideas, dreams, and expectations of success. Usually, however, the honeymoon is over before we can really start enjoying our new jobs. The first few days, weeks, and sometimes months can be very positive with a new company and new relationships. But many times, the reality of the position, what the job requires and the unspoken expectations of our superiors, can be discouraging.

The best way to start a new job and have the best chance to succeed is to start with an open line of communication with your boss or other leaders. When you come into the job with the basic expectations of working hard, know that the real job doesn't start until after a few days or weeks. Realizing that there will be some difficult days ahead, you will not be disappointed with your new job.

Another key to success in your job, once the initial period of learning and getting used to the new company is past, is to take opportunities and challenges that present themselves so you can continue to learn. Many times these opportunities give you visibility in the rest of the company, allow you to form new relationships, and expand your horizons within the company and even beyond. Sometimes, because of your involvement in unexpected projects or impromptu meetings, you might be considered for other positions you were not even thinking about when you first started at your current job.

During the course of months and years, however, you can become disillusioned with your job and feel discouraged. There may be many reasons to feel this way. One reason may be that the job is not really what you expected or what they described when you first signed up. Another reason is that you have outgrown your job. You have learned everything there was to learn and now you don't feel any new challenges to keep you going. Sometimes, you may be extremely busy, but the job is very routine, and repetitive tasks bore you. If you are the kind of person who likes variety, you need to find jobs that provide you with an assortment of tasks, or become involved with other company activities that may fulfill that need.

The question is, what do you do when you feel you have lost your purpose? What do you do when you don't see why you are in the position you are in currently, and you no longer see the value you provide to your organization? In my opinion, it takes awhile to get to this point. Therefore, watch for early signs of discouragement or feelings that you're losing the purpose of being there.

How can you find out early so you don't get to the point when it's too late and all of the sudden you hate the job you're in? There are several things you can do to avoid discouragement in your job or losing your purpose. Ask yourself these questions:

1. Why am I here in this job at this time in my life?
2. What are the things I like about my current job?
3. What are the things I dislike in this job?
4. Why did I accept this job to begin with?
5. Is the company I work for doing what they told me they do? Are they following their own mission and vision?
6. Are the leaders of this company honest and truthful about caring about their employees and customers?
7. Are there other things I should be doing or learning that I'm not?
8. What is my value to this organization?
9. Why is it important that my job gets done on time and right every time?
10. Where do I go from here?

These questions may be hard to answer, but you need to be true to yourself and keep asking them often, so you are aware at all times of your purpose. From the spiritual perspective, are you being a light in this company? Are you being a good example to others of living a Christian life? Are you using the gifts God gave you in this job?

When you go back to God to ask these kinds of questions, He will give you the answer you are seeking. He will direct your path. He will give you new ideas about how to become involved in new activities, learn new ways of doing your current job, and connect you with the right people at your company who will help you or give you advice.

When you have an open line of communication with your boss or supervisor, you can approach that person and share some of your feelings. Ask what your boss sees as your value to the organization. Ask for feedback on how you're doing even if it's not time for your annual review. Your boss will appreciate that you are concerned about your contribution to the company and your interest in succeeding in your job. Sometimes, employees don't approach their managers for fear of interrupting them or simply because they feel intimidated. However, most supervisors and managers are happy to help their employees and will welcome the opportunity to get to know them better. Most leaders want their team to succeed and are open to new ideas on how to help them improve and stay challenged. If you share with your boss from the beginning that you are the kind of person who likes to continually learn, your boss will probably be looking to give you extra projects or new things to learn on an ongoing basis. If you are a good employee, your boss won't want to lose you. It is costly for companies to continually train new employees. Most companies would rather invest in their current team and develop them so employees can bring more of their gifts and contributions to their jobs.

Don't despair, when you feel you've lost the purpose in your job, go to God first, ask Him for the answers and you shall find them. Search your heart and ask God to help you find the right job where your life's purpose and calling will align with your job. Surround yourself with positive people who will encourage you when you are down and appreciate you as a person, not only as a coworker. Choose to work for companies that appreciate their employees and value their input and effort. Create and maintain a successful relationship with your boss so you can later share how you feel and your boss can give you advice.

Most importantly, you have a purpose in your life. You need to find that purpose by seeking God first. Then you will never lose your purpose at work.

ISAIAH 49:4 (NLT) *I replied, "But my work seems so useless! I have spent my strength for nothing and to no purpose at all. Yet I leave it all in the Lord's hand; I will trust God for my reward."*

- **QUESTIONS TO PONDER**
  1. What is your purpose in your current job?
  2. What warning signs do you recognize when losing your purpose in your job?
  3. In what ways does your purpose in life align with your job?

- **ACTION ITEMS**
  1. Write down your role in your current job. This may help you identify your purpose there.
  2. Seek input from your manager regarding your value to the organization.
  3. If you have not found your purpose yet, ask God and He will help you find it.

Chapter 16

What Will Your Legacy Be?

*W*ebster's Dictionary describes legacy as anything handed down from the past from an ancestor or predecessor. Synonyms are inheritance and heritage. Inheritance usually refers to something material, such as a piece of property, passed down from parents to their children. Heritage refers to other, nonmaterial things passed down from generation to generation, such as culture, moral and ethical standards, and beliefs. I believe we all leave a legacy, whether we intend to or not. Just as we influence people during the course of our lives, and that influence can be positive or negative, we leave a legacy that will be remembered in a positive or negative way. We create our legacy with what we do every day of our lives here on earth. We leave a legacy also through our children. They inherit not only our material possessions, if any, but also our morals, some characteristics, and what they learned from us by our examples.

You have a choice to make every day that you go to work. Will what you do today help you create a legacy you will be proud of leaving some day? Even if you don't think of staying with a company for the rest of your life, you still need to consider what legacy you will leave behind when you leave that company. That's why it's so important not to burn bridges when you leave a company. You never know if you will be working with some of those same people again, or if they will buy the next company you will be working for. When you get a promotion to a new department within your company, don't leave your friendships behind. Keep your network of friends and acquaintances. Someone from your old department may later become your boss or your employee. If you switch companies within the same industry, you, for sure, want to keep your network, because people within the same industry tend to move around and work at the same companies. If you move to a new industry, you may still need your old connections, in case you don't like the new field you moved into.

The main question to answer is: do you really want to leave a positive legacy? Most people would say, "of course." So then, how do you want to be remembered? This doesn't necessarily mean being remembered only when you die, but during the course of your life, throughout your career, and during your working life. When you leave a company or a previous job within the same company, what do you want people to say when they talk about you? Do you want people to say, "Oh yes, that was a person who cared about others"? Or do you want them to say, "Oh, I don't even want to think about that person! That was the worst manager I ever had"?

I believe when we think of others first and find purpose in our work, the positive legacy we leave behind will happen naturally. We don't have to worry about what to do or what to say when. We simply care for and about others, and people notice. When we walk in God's will for our lives, He will make sure our legacy is written following our path of life so others can read it as they follow. Our legacy when we are alive is our reputation. Our reputation is simply what others think of us. We build our reputation by our actions—what we say and do—every day. Unfortunately, once we build a bad reputation, it is very hard to change it, so we need to be careful to build and keep a good reputation for ourselves.

How do you leave a legacy or create a good reputation while you are in the job you are right now? Think daily of how you can improve the way you do your work. Think of new ways to carry out the processes you're involved with. Help others succeed in their jobs by helping them in any way you can. Develop new alliances between departments so your company works internally together more efficiently.

Establish good relationships with leadership and sincerely care for them and the company you work for. Those leaders are the ones who first believed in you to do the job you were hired to do. Find the reason you are in your current job right now. Learn new things so you become a more informed employee and knowledgeable team member. Be an instrument of unity rather than division amongst your coworkers. Respect your employees, your coworkers, and your leaders. As you do all these things, you are establishing a good reputation for yourself and an environment of trust where people can flourish.

Take ownership in the company you work for and appropriate the company's future. Learn the vision and mission of your company. If you are the founder, write the vision and mission of your company, if you have not done so yet. Ask yourself the question, what am I doing to fulfill the vision of this company? Treat the company and everything in it (the employees, vendors, assets, and liabilities) as your own. When you do, you will start to see a difference on how you behave toward the people in the company you work for. You will start defending your workplace when others say bad things about it. You will stop complaining about the things you don't like (and actually start doing something about those things you want to change), and you will start feeling like you belong. The tasks you do in your job will suddenly make sense, and you will see how they fit in the big picture. Understanding how all the pieces come together and how what you do integrates into the entire company is easier to do in a small organization, but it can be done in a big company as well.

The main points to understand include the concept of caring about the company you work for, taking ownership of the company that hired you, and having a feeling of belonging once you take ownership. It is crucial to have an understanding of how important your job is, no matter what it is. Understanding the concept of ownership means being thankful for the job you have, thanking God for it, and giving Him all the glory for what you do—working as unto the Lord. These are all ways you leave a positive legacy wherever you go and at the end of your life.

PSALM 16:5 (NLT) *Lord, you alone are my inheritance, my cup of blessing. You guard all that is mine.*

- **QUESTIONS TO PONDER**

  1. What is your legacy?
  2. What bridges do you have to repair or relationships to fix?
  3. What part do you play in your company? What ownership do you feel?

- **ACTION ITEMS**

  1. Start taking ownership of the company you work for today.
  2. Make a new connection to improve relationships between two areas of your company.
  3. Thank God for your job, and ask Him to help you understand your importance in that company.

Chapter 17

The End of *This* Road

As I shared in Chapter 10, *How I Found a Purpose in Every Job*, I left a secure job at a nonprofit (church) to start a bank with my former boss who was also my mentor and friend. In this chapter, I want to share more and expand how the bank startup came to be.

I had never thought of starting a bank. This was my friend's dream, and I wanted to help him achieve his dream—that was my mission. During the summer of 2004, my former boss and I started conversations about starting a new bank, a "De Novo" Bank. He had four potential groups of investors with whom he could start a bank. On September 7, he made a decision to go with a particular group of investors. On that same day, while praying about my next move, I felt God leading me to call my friend to give him my final decision. I told him, "I am ready to go back to banking, but this time I don't want to be in lending. I want to be the CFO of the bank and learn to run the bank as a business."

He answered, "Deal."

It wasn't until months later that we compared our calendars and realized God was directing us both to start this bank together. We call it our "September 7 story."

We did preliminary work on the bank startup without getting paid during the last three months of 2004, at nights and on the weekends, while I was still working at the church. On January 2, 2005 we both officially started working (getting paid) on starting the bank. I remember clearly one afternoon, sitting at my dining room table and asking myself, "How the heck do you start a bank? Lord, are you sure you want me to do this? I have no idea where to start!"

Then God gave me an idea: treat it as a huge project and break it into small pieces—one department, one area at a time. So I purchased Microsoft Project and made a checklist of everything I knew we would need, based on what I learned in my previous thirteen years in banking, plus the five years of having worked at the church leading Finance, Human Resources, and IT.

The first question my boss and I had was, "How are we going to get paid?"

Well, let's set up payroll first.

Our second question was, "We need health insurance. How do we get that set up?"

Okay, let's figure out that one next. Since he is about nineteen years older than me, he was interested in retirement, so he asked me to "set something up for 401K so we can have that as our best benefit for the bank." So I did.

When I was done writing the list of items we needed to accomplish before opening the bank, we had seventeen pages and 516 tasks to do! Some of my tasks took me one hour, and the biggest item took me sixty hours to set up.

The process of starting a bank is an amazing experience—one that not many bankers get to experience in their lives, and especially as an immigrant. What an opportunity my friend gave me. He believed in me and knew that I could do it. I led the team that set up the infrastructure of the bank, covering all the backbone areas, such as Finance/Budgets/Accounting, IT, HR, Operations, Compliance, Internal Audit, Office Management, and everything in between. He worked with the original investors to form the board of directors and to raise the almost eleven million dollars in capital we needed to start the bank.

During the first six months, we were paid from the newly formed holding company, which is the parent company of the bank. The funding for the startup costs came from a loan to the holding company from the original investors.

Someday I will write another book on how to start a bank from scratch. I will include all the steps as well as the emotional part of my life that went along with the process. For now, I will focus on the experience of moving on after completing my mission of starting this bank and help grow it successfully.

As I shared before, during those nine years, I was promoted several times, from VP Operations and CFO to SVP, then EVP and COO/CFO. My last role at the bank was as EVP/COO and CRO (chief risk officer). As the bank grew, and we were able to hire more employees, I was able to delegate functions. As I trained others in the various jobs, I was able to continue to learn new things that now applied to the larger bank. At the same time, new regulations continued to come out. We had to learn them, adjust to them, create new policies and procedures to comply, and train the rest of the staff.

In February 2010, the board of directors implemented their succession plan and my original boss, the founding president and CEO of the bank was no longer my boss. I now had a new boss and had to build that relationship. As with any new leadership change, other things started to change. Some things were good, and some were not. The management team also grew and nothing was "the way it used to be" when we started the bank. That was hard for me to accept, but I went along with all the changes. The bank was going through growing pains, and I felt every one of them. My original boss stayed on in a new role, and we continued working together with the shareholders, so that was good.

In December 2012, I made a list of all my "annual duties," and I realized I didn't even need a checklist. I had them memorized! This realization was scary to me because, in my opinion and as a learner, I thought to myself, *If I can memorize my annual duties that means I've done them too many times … I'm not learning anymore.*

I almost panicked, but the busyness of the New Year with the financials, budgets, regulatory exams, shareholder transactions, company taxes, etc., kept me away from thinking deeper into this concern. I thought, *Well, I will just keep myself busy and I'm sure I'll find something new to learn soon.* But the months kept going by, and I was getting bored.

The volume of work continued to increase but with no new responsibilities. Then I thought to start focusing on the area of Risk Management. I requested that my job as CFO/COO be split when the bank grew to 250 million dollars in assets, which happened at the end of 2013. In December 2013, I was able to promote all my employees to the next level in their careers. At this point, they all had employees under them, and I was no longer the backup for anyone. I was finally *overseeing* versus *doing*. Although it felt liberating, and

I could have continued on this position easily, as a learner, I needed a new challenge. From the spiritual perspective, I felt God calling me to my next chapter in life.

I decided it was time to part ways. I told the staff, when I announced it at the staff meeting on September 17, 2014, "My kids at home grew up, and my kids at work grew up. I hired the right people. I fired the right people. I built teams. I trained you all. I promoted you several times and helped you get where you are now as leaders of your own departments. All my ducks are in a row. I leave you with a well-oiled machine. My mission here is complete." I went on to share what I planned to do next, which was to pursue my dreams—ALL of them!

A couple of days after I made the announcement, I was biking with my husband, and the Lord put in my heart to write this chapter. I knew then that's why I hadn't been able to finish this book. I was missing the last chapter. I was first going to title it "The End of *the* Road." But the Lord made me realize that this was not the end of *the* road, just the end of *this* road in my life. There was a brand new road that He was preparing for me, and I didn't know it. I tend to hang onto where I'm comfortable, safe, and secure. At the same time, I cannot coast and stay at a place where I'm not being challenged. It was a horrible internal struggle that took me one year to unravel and untangle. This bank was my baby. My employees were like my kids, regardless of their ages. I loved these people. Of the forty-three employees that the bank had at the time, I hired them all except probably the last three or four when the HR department stopped reporting to me early in the year.

So here I am, following my heart and pursuing my dreams. I decided to start a bank consulting practice and also to pursue my public speaking career. I find it interesting that starting my own business has never been a dream of mine. However, I feel that in order to pursue all my dreams, I need to have the freedom and flexibility that comes with owning my own business. Only God knows if this business will be successful, but I will give it my all and my best. I will apply all the knowledge that I acquired over the past twenty-nine years since I came to the United States. I will apply all the experience I gained in banking and how to run a bank as a business, and use the gifts and talents that God gave me to help others be successful. I will nurture the fire within me.

I will use all my gifts and connect them to my unique calling of God in my life. I hope reading about my life experiences helps you find your gifts, discover your calling, and finally connect the two. It is only when we are in God's unique will for our lives that we will be completely fulfilled and have a positive impact on those around us. I encourage you to pursue your calling. Find your gifts. Connect the two, and light your fire within!

HEBREWS 11:1, 6 (NLT) *What is faith? It is the confident assurance that what we hope for is going to happen. It is the evidence of things we cannot yet see ... So, you see, it is impossible to please God without faith. Anyone who wants to come to him must believe that there is a God and that he rewards those who sincerely seek him.*

- **QUESTIONS TO PONDER**

  1. Did the ideas in this book cause you to discover any of your gifts or look at any of your gifts in a new way?
  2. In what ways have you discovered your unique calling of God in your life?
  3. What steps are you taking to connect your gifts with your calling?

- **ACTION ITEMS**

  1. Share the list of gifts you have with a friend you trust.
  2. Share your calling with someone you trust.
  3. Choose activities where you are connecting your gifts to your calling. Let your fire burn bright!

EPILOGUE

I hope this book took you on a journey of reflection, gratitude, and discovery. God made you unique and He gave you special gifts. When you embark on a journey of discovering what your gifts are, you will find them. Then going through the process of polishing those gifts will be very rewarding. Lastly, actually using all your gifts throughout your life is one of the most fulfilling experiences you can have.

It is in my heart that this book serves as an energizing tool to help you get started in discovering your gifts and connecting them to your calling and purpose in your life. It all starts with your desire to fulfill the call of God in your life and wanting to use the gifts and talents He gave you to advance His Kingdom.

ACKNOWLEDGMENTS

I thank all my friends and colleagues who inspired me to write this book. I first thank my beloved husband Tim who is always there for me and supports me as I fulfill the calling of God in my life. I thank my friends Reid Evenson, Shawn Carlson, Barry Sorensen, Todd Mathison, Laura Adams, and Keith Adams who read the first unedited version of this book and gave me their sincere input and feedback so it can help readers discover their gifts and connect them to their calling.

Special thanks to my long-time mentor and dear friend, Esperanza Guerrero-Anderson. Throughout my career she has helped me navigate in my mission field: corporate America. She encouraged me when I was down and celebrated my successes, too. Special thanks to my other long-time mentor and friend, Reid Evenson. He gave me the opportunity to work with him in cash management when I was a teller at the beginning of my banking career. He is also the one who believed in me and gave me the amazing opportunity to start a bank.

It is because of people like Esperanza and Reid and their contributions and influence in my life that I have been able to succeed in my career. I only hope to pay forward their kindness and impact many people throughout my life just as they have. I have deep admiration and respect for the two of them and will forever be grateful. Thank you for believing in me!

ABOUT THE AUTHOR

Marcia (Marci) Malzahn is a wife, mother, writer, author, and speaker as well as a successful executive, entrepreneur, and professional. She started three businesses, climbed the corporate ladder, and has experience both in the for-profit and the nonprofit world. Marcia is president of Malzahn Strategic, a bank management consulting practice that works with community banks that need strategic planning, enterprise risk management, and talent management expertise and support.

Considered a business leader in the Minneapolis/St. Paul community, Marcia was the recipient of several awards including "25 On the Rise," given by the Minnesota Hispanic Chamber of Commerce to successful Minnesota Hispanics under age forty. *Minneapolis/St. Paul Business Journal* named her one of the "40 Under Forty." *Finance and Commerce* newspaper named her one of the "Top Women in Finance," and *Northwestern Financial Review Magazine* gave her the "Outstanding Women in Banking" Award.

Marcia is the author of *Devotions for Working Women: A Daily Inspiration to Live a Successful and Balanced Life* (Expert Publishing, Inc., 2006). Marcia holds a BA in Business Management from Bethel University and is also a graduate of the Graduate School of Banking, Madison, Wisconsin.

Marcia's mission is to help others in the workplace be successful in every area of their lives. She and her husband Tim live in Minnesota and have two grown children, Nicole and Patrick.